My Dogs, MS and Me

Emma Coldron

Contents

Preface

As I entered our kitchen to the hustle and bustle of early morning TV, breakfast and pots, I saw only one thing; the five squirming bundles of fur. My mum was taking care of a border terrier and her five puppies during weekdays for her boss. This is where it all began, my one true love; dogs.

I would sit for hours with the pups, holding them as they snuggled into my warm neck. Naturally my brother and I named them all and genuinely fell in love with each and every one.

When summer was nearly over so too was my time with the pups and one by one the puppies' new owners came to take them home. It was getting dark and there was one pup left, the only boy, sitting all alone looking very small in a big blue bed. "Mum when is Bruno's owner coming to get him?" I asked wanting to know how much precious time I had left with him. "Well," she said with a smile "they're already here." Slowly it sank in that he was ours and my brother and I were so happy.

That night as mum came to say goodnight she told me that Bruno would whine but I must not get up to him, that he needed to get used to being alone at night time. So that night after mum and dad had gone to bed and the little boy started to cry for his littermates, I tiptoed out of my room, down the hall and into the kitchen. I sat on the floor in front of his bed and lay half in it with my arms around him until he fell asleep, then I tiptoed back to my bed.

Thirteen years later

Tears rolled down my face; they just kept coming. MS. Visions of wheelchairs and hospital beds consumed my thoughts. Why me? A cold wet nose nuzzled under my hand and licked my salty palms. My fingertips found their way on to Megan's soft, warm head. Her big brown eyes found mine and there was a moment of stillness. Then my beautiful cocker spaniel took her paw and placed it softly on my knee, and I knew; I wasn't alone.

Chapter 1

Ten years later.

"Dave!

Look there's some Jack Russell puppies in the paper!" As my boyfriend entered our living room he had that look on his face. The 'oh I know what's coming next' look. "Could we go and see them, just to have a look, we don't have to get one, pleeeease?!"

Dave and I had been together for three years, this time around. I'd known him since I was fifteen, he was a couple of years older, and back then we met by chance, and went on to have a beautiful, head in the clouds, teenage romance. It was one of those forbidden loves that pulls you both together and cocoons you in dreams and devotion. We were from completely different walks of life. Our two families could not have been more different, I thought of us as a modern day Romeo and Juliet.

It did, of course, end in tragedy and he broke my heart. He never left my thoughts, nor I his, and it wasn't long before we crossed paths again. In fact we crossed paths a few times before I let him back into my life but you know things are meant to be if the universe just keeps setting the two of you up.

We found living the dream; the house, the jobs, the car, to be far removed from our ideas and memories but we were living it and while life apparently was not a teenage dream, it was full of potential and glimpses of paradise.

Dave was a Decorator for a big firm in our town and I worked in childcare. We didn't have a lot of money but we always had enough.

We had been talking about getting a dog for a few months. Our teenage dream had always included our very own dog. We were renting our own place, a two up two down townhouse with a small garden and I was in between jobs meaning I was at home to settle a dog in; so it seemed as good a time as any. The problem was I wanted a Border Terrier and Dave wanted a British Bulldog, so we compromised on Ronnie.

I'd always wanted a Jack Russell to name after my grandad; he'd always had them when he was alive. We did all the recommended research on the breed, but the warnings of Jack Russell's being prone to aggression, barking and disliking children were all excused; 'that won't happen to our puppy'.

"Ok if that's what you really want, but I'm not guaranteeing getting one, just as long as you know." Dave raised his blonde eyebrows at me. I replied with attempting to conceal an incredibly ecstatic smile.

I'd phoned the number and spoken to the owner; he'd given us the directions and we drove across town to what we knew was a less than desirable area. (Some people just don't know a sign when they see one!) We kept looking at each other, I had so much excitement fluttering around in my tummy, but I had to try and hold it in because we were 'only going to have a look', although judging by the look on Dave's face I wasn't fooling him; nor him me, for that matter.

We pulled up to the terraced house and I couldn't knock on the door fast enough. A middle aged man answered the door. He was wearing a tradesman's uniform and had obviously just arrived home.

"Come in you must be Emma," the man stood aside and welcomed us in. As soon as I entered the small family kitchen I saw them. They were in a wire pen under the work top in a space made for a fridge or washing machine. There were four of them, two were tan and white and two were black white and tan. They were so small, about the size of Dave's hand. They, quite simply, were adorable.

I did notice however that they were on their own in the pen with nothing but newspaper. My heart strings were being pulled for the poor tiny babies. "Where is their mum?" I asked the man.

"Oh she's out here with my other two dogs", he walked over to the back door and opened it, and I saw a kennel with three Jack Russells inside.

"The tan and white one is their mum, the black and tan is the dad and the black and white one is one I rescued; he's a bit snappy so I won't let them out." (Yet another ignored sign.) All three of the dogs were barking uncontrollably at us, especially the mum. I imagine she wanted us away from her babies.

"The mother does come in to her pups though doesn't she?" I asked with trepidation.

"Oh yes they all come in in the evening when we get home from work", the man answered. Despite all the signs there wasn't an ounce of me that wanted to walk away without securing sharing a future with one of these puppies. I passed one of the puppies to Dave and saw his face melt as it snuggled into his chest.

Two weeks later, far too early as the pups were only six weeks old; we travelled back to the breeder's house with our cardboard box and blanket to collect our boy. We had chosen one of the black white and tan pups as I'd never seen a Jack with those markings. When we got there it was even worse than last time. The pups were literally rolling in their own filth. But it didn't stop me picking up my Ronnie and holding him close. I noticed a white marking on his back that I hadn't noticed the first time – emotions were running high that day so all I'd really seen was his beautiful face - the mark was as though someone had dabbed him with the paintbrush. Dave being the painter and decorator was chuffed to bits with this little omen.

We put Ronnie in the box and said our goodbyes and were on our way. I felt so awful leaving the remaining two pups behind although the other male had already found his lucky escape. Ronnie wasn't too fazed about the car he just sat with his front paws resting on top of the box looking at us both.

"Hey there boy, are you coming home with us?" For saying I had to persuade him into this, Dave was smitten.

As soon as we got home I looked down into Ronnie's eyes and said; "I'm sorry boy but you have just got to have a bath." So, as if leaving everything he's ever known wasn't trauma enough, his lovely new owners then doused him in water and baby shampoo. I think Ronnie and bath time will always have a difficult relationship from now on.

He settled in straight away. We'd bought him a little red bed and he curled up and slept...and slept...and slept.

"Emma! Will you leave that puppy alone," I heard Dave bellow from the living room. I had made my umpteenth trip to the kitchen floor to cuddle and fuss over my sleepy boy. I felt like a kid on Christmas day and couldn't contain myself. Ronnie had been in my life for four hours and I already loved him with every beat of my heart.

It was Ronnie's second night with us and we had to go out for an hour or two to one of the local pubs for Dave's sister's birthday. The thought of being anywhere but with Dave and Ronnie in our own little puppy bubble had little appeal to me.

As I brushed the blush onto my cheeks the girl in the mirror did not have the usual 'I'm going out on the town' twinkle in her eye. Dave appeared behind me and resting his hands on my shoulders, nuzzled into my neck.

"Hey there pretty lady," he mumbled through kisses.

"Why thank you, you don't scrub up to bad yourself," I smiled back at him through the reflection.

Downstairs a little boy looked at me with big soft eyes.

"Oh Dave I don't want to go," I said with a protruding bottom lip.

"Come on, two hours that's all. Get your shoes on madam," Dave said with a firm smile.

Our house at the time was open plan, so we improvised by blocking off the kitchen with an ironing board, amongst other things. We checked and checked again, no, no way that our tiny pup can get over that.

"Emma he'll be fine," Dave said to me as he saw my face as I locked the door. But his reassurances didn't ease the wrench in my stomach as I left my tiny pup and walked into town.

As I sat beside Dave on a sofa in the noisy pub, all I could think about was my little boy and on the way back I practically ran. I opened the door and poked my head around the corner into the kitchen. I could see his bed, his bowls, his toys, but no Ronnie.

"Dave he's not in here! Oh my god where is he? I knew I shouldn't have left him!" My voice carried the shriek of panic.

"Calm down Em he can't be far," Dave said with his composed as ever attitude.

As my heart pounded with anxiety I jumped over the ironing board fence and desperately searched down the side of the fridge, which was absolutely the only place he could be. Just as Dave and I started to pull the fridge out Ronnie came bounding in from the Lounge. He cocked his head to one side and looked at us stood in the kitchen as if to say 'what on earth are you two doing in there?'

Chapter 2

The power of a smile; fighting depression with man's best friend.

Before long I had a job, in a nursery again which I wasn't ecstatic about but the bills needed paying. The childcare scene was really beginning to bore me. After five years of children spitting in your face and staff too busy gossiping and eating McDonalds to pick up a crying child, the rewards were dwarfed by the downside.

I hated leaving Ronnie. I had spent all day every day with him for a month and now I had to leave his big heartbroken eyes every day. The nursery was ok at first but as the days went on the same patterns emerged. Staff would rather sit gossip and stuff their faces than make a difference to these children's lives. In addition, the manager made a daily habit of bullying one of the staff. Basically, it was hell.

Dave and I were making dinner. I thought to myself - I've got to tell him. I can't go back there; life's too short to feel like this, isn't it?

"Dave this job, I don't think I can go anymore."

Dave stopped chopping the carrot in his hand.

"What? What do you mean?" Why?"

"I told you, it's just awful I can't stand it."

"You can't just leave we don't have enough money as it is." A look of panic and confusion filled his blue eyes. "I know you don't really like it but I hate my job too, my boss is an idiot but that's what it's like everywhere Em."

A hopeless feeling filled my chest. How could I explain it wasn't just that I didn't like it, it was that the feeling of being in the same room as those people made my heart pump faster and I felt like I was thirteen again. I'd suffered at the hands of bullies in secondary school; it was the worst time of my life. The feeling I got in this nursery's community of staff was like being back in the classroom. Maybe he was right maybe I just needed to grow up and get on with it.

"Never mind, I'll just look for another job and keep going for now. I know we need the money, I just feel pretty desperate. I really hate it Dave." I looked at him and his eyes softened.

"Well if you hate it that much then yeah just look for a new job and then there's a light at the end of the tunnel isn't there. But we really need your wages babe. Especially now we have this puppy you wanted and continue to spoil." A smile crept on his face as he looked over at Ronnie, who was curled up in another brand new blanket surrounded by toys and bones. Just looking at my boy made the thought of going back there, a little easier to bear. I loved this tiny dog so much and having him in our life just made me keep smiling.

- - - - -

I decided to take Ronnie into work. Perhaps it would make me feel a little more included, plus seeing the children would be good socialisation for him. Unfortunately one of the children, a Polish little boy, was so excited he screamed in Ronnie's face, he just didn't have the words to express his happiness so a screaming smile it was and this obviously terrified poor Ronnie as his eyes widened and he struggled to get away. I passed him to one of the other girls for a second and he yelped with fear. I quickly took him back and after he had calmed down I tried again with a different girl. Ronnie settled into her arms and fell asleep – this was the girl everyone else was bullying – I thought to myself; that's my boy.

Around a week later the feelings inside me had intensified tenfold. The idea I would be the next bullying victim consumed every thought I had. I couldn't control it however much I tried.

It was after dinner and time to go back to work. I gave Ronnie the biggest cuddle and as I locked up the house something inside me had shifted. It felt as though the bubble of anxiety I'd had, had burst and found its way into every part of my body. Everywhere felt heavy and as I walked back to the nursery, it was like walking in treacle. The rest of the day people asked; "What's wrong with you?"

To which I replied; "Oh I just don't feel very well," as I struggled to breath in and out and not collapse in a heap of desperation. That was the last day I went there; it broke me and depression hit me like a double decker bus. I would just stare at the wall or hide under a blanket and cry uncontrollably. I felt as though the whole world was just happening around me. I felt I had no control over what happened to me day to day and that made me feel truly hopeless and trapped.

The doctors diagnosed Anxiety and Depression and I started a course of anti depressants and counselling. I was signed off work with stress so I didn't have to go back to that hellhole and the saviour that is my grandma helped us out with money for that initial stage.

Dave couldn't comprehend where his girlfriend had gone. Our relationship seemed to have crumbled overnight along with every other part of my life. We rowed almost constantly as every molehill was a mountain to me. Not that they were all my fault; obviously being a man Dave was responsible for at least 90 % of the rows. In all seriousness it's a miracle we made it through that and a lot of it was down to Ronnie.

During those long days home alone when the world seemed so daunting, I don't know if I'd have made it out of the dark without my four legged angel. I'd wake up and just want to pull the duvet over my head and disappear for the day, but I had a puppy downstairs that needed a wee and his breakfast. So up I'd get and as I walked down the stairs I'd hear him jumping up against the wooden gate on the kitchen. Some days I'd come down to a lovely clean boy eager to lather me with kisses. Other days I'd come down to him jumping ever so happily in his own poop. He'd be stinking and be just as eager to kiss and cuddle his mummy. As I cleaned him up his little face would just say 'oh no not another wash mum!' Those mornings I'd have woken up in a black place, yet the antics of my puppy created a faint, but powerful smile.

Then there was the chore of getting dressed which was made much more animated by Ronnie's determined efforts to pull off my socks as I put them on. This sounds very irritating but when a tiny little puppy is pledging full on war with a sock you just can't help but laugh, which at the time was a much needed medicine. On the occasions he won the sock war he'd run off with it under the bed, right in the middle where he knew I couldn't reach him and proceed to yap with self satisfaction.

He made me smile in so many ways. Our stairs had open banisters and if Ronnie was upstairs and we shouted him, his head would appear through the railings – the floating head we called him. That was also his chosen spot for keeping watch of his territory boundaries and seeing off anyone who dared to cross them with ferocious yapping. If only he would learn what was danger and what was the postman our house would be much quieter.

After a few weeks of medication and Ronnie therapy I was back in the land of the living. I'd started a new job with a lovely small team of staff and things seemed to finally be back on track.

Chapter 3

Ronnie's Aggression and Enter Tess!

"Ronnie! No stop it!" I yanked him back by his lead as he barked with aggression at a passing dog. I smiled apologetically at the woman walking a very well mannered Labrador. Embarrassment flushed to my face.

During the time I was off work with depression Ronnie had started to display these signs of aggression. But he was so small and cute it was hard not to laugh at his attempts to be menacing to passersby and dogs ten times his size. It was certainly proving to be no laughing matter.

I don't know when the idea planted itself firmly in my mind but I thought, perhaps getting another dog would cure Ronnie of his dislike of his fellow canines. I made a call to the local RSPCA kennels after deciding we'd prefer to rescue one. When I say 'we' that would insinuate Dave was fully on board with the idea of a second dog and he definitely wasn't. But I was only having a look wasn't I?

The RSPCA said they had another Jack Russell (yes another one) and she was very unhappy in the kennels. I knew she wasn't lying because I could hear her wailing down the phone. The woman said I was welcome to bring Ronnie down to meet her.

I was so excited even at the prospect of meeting her; I phoned my mum and arranged to meet her at the rescue kennels in a few hours. My Mum is a wonderful woman. She is strong, independent, a doting wife and mother and works hard for what she has. She is a little like her daughter, or should I say I'm a little like her, in regard to having strong opinions. Mum's strong opinion on me getting a second dog was; 'oh no you're not!'

I looked out my car window at the rural view. I loved the countryside, the green fields and openness filled me with calm. One day I will live in a little white cottage surrounded by fields, I thought to myself, where Ronnie can run freely and Dave and I can raise our child in the beauty of nature. I snapped myself back from my dream and turned off the country lane and down a long drive to discover a pack of dogs of all shapes and sizes in the middle, following a man's every move, without leads! So it isn't just Ceaser Milan then, I thought, perhaps there was hope for me yet.

I parked the car and turned to my back seat where Ronnie was sitting in his crate. His big dark eyes looked at me as if asking for some sort of explanation, his ears pricked to attention, he was ready for action; whatever it may be.

"Ronnie we are going to get you a friend, now do please try not to eat her."

I put on his lead and walked over to my mum who had already arrived, together we made our way up to the kennels. As we did so mum said; "Now remember you don't have to take her home, just meet her then go home and think about it."

Behind the counter was the lovely young girl I'd spoken to on the phone. As she went to get the dog; Tess was her name, I was practically dancing with excitement; Ronnie on the other hand was completely blasé about the whole thing.

"Ronnie!" I screamed, as he cocked his leg up a bag of dog food; which, apparently, I was buying.

The door opened and the kennel maid brought her out. The little dog was all white except for a black face and big black pointy ears. She danced around on the other end of the lead whining loudly with excitement. Despite her looking and sounding very happy, her eyes looked so desperate and sad; I imagine she must have been thinking 'are you going to take me home and love me? Please get me out of here?' She was definitely in need of a cuddle which my mum gladly gave her; my grounded partner in this excursion had now crumbled.

"Oh look at her," she said as the little dog climbed up on to her lap and lathered her with kisses.

I had Ronnie on his lead and his body language and face said it all 'what in God's name is that and why am I so close to it?' But the kennel maid helped us introduce them and 20 minutes later they were running around playing together. The manager of the kennels suggested we take her for a trial for the weekend. I thought at this point I really should call Dave.

Reluctantly he agreed, though he must have stressed ten times it was only for the weekend. So mum and I drove home with a dog each, apparently my journey with Ronnie was much quieter than hers. It appeared poor Tess wasn't very good in a car.

After a while we had to pop out so I put Tess in Ronnie's crate with a blanket and off we went. About an hour later my phone rang. As I looked at the caller display I smiled; Dave.

"I've met the dog," his voice was laced with an underlying dissatisfaction.

"I came in from work and she had pooed all over the cage and rolled in it too. So I was greeted with the lovely task of cleaning that up."

"Oh. Oh dear, that's completely my fault I shouldn't have left her I'm really sorry baby." I thought 'oh Tess come on work with me here!'

When I got back Dave didn't seem to mind the earlier incident and in fact he and Tess seemed to have really taken to one another and sat cuddling on the sofa. Ronnie was in love with her too and they would play for hours then snuggle up together for a nap. By the time the weekend was over it was plain to see Tess was already part of our little family.

So that was that; Tess never went back and became dog number two. For about three weeks Tess was the model dog; she became house trained in two days, did anything we asked and gave the best cosy cuddles. The only apparent problem was the fact she wailed at the top of her voice if we went upstairs without her. The poor little girl was so scared to be alone, I presume, in case she got left behind again.

Then there was Tess' first walk. We took her and Ronnie to a big park full of fields, people, children, other dogs, lakes, squirrels. Well it was all too much for Tess – she was just so happy, although to everyone else in the entire park it sounded as though we were killing our dog. She absolutely wailed with excitement, everywhere she looked there was something to make her even happier. It was the most embarrassing but funniest half an hour of my life. I'm pretty sure that was Tess' first ever walk.

Things with Tess calmed down and we all got into the stride of life again. On one of our many walks Tess and I turned the corner down the path to the park to find a group of people stood chatting, their dogs running freely around them. Well, one of the dogs, a black Labrador, decided he didn't like the look of Tess at all and lunged at us barking; Tess put her tail between her legs and cowered.

"Please," I shouted, "get your dog!" The woman got him under control before any damage was done and we carried on with our walk. But that was the end of Tess the well behaved dog. She decided from this moment on that attack was the best form of defence, with a bit of help from her older brother Ronnie. So now I had two aggressive dogs to walk every day.

It was hell. The way people looked at you, was as if you had a savage Lion on the end of your lead. They'd pick up their little dogs, cross the road and stare in horror. I would hold on to their leads for dear life as we passed other dogs, bin men, postmen, bikes, trailers and just about anything else that moved. I would just get from A to B as fast as possible. What happened to having a dog for long relaxing walks in the park? I was coming home after some walks and just crying in desperation. So I decided enough was enough; time to call in a professional.

Chapter 4

Call in the Cavalry

"Em, come on, can we really afford a dog trainer?" Dave turned to me as I sat scouring the phone book.

"Babe we don't have a choice they are unruly!" My voice began to rise. "I can't take another day of walking down the road, my arms being pulled out my sockets and dying inside as they bark and bark at anyone I walk past! It's humiliating!" My eyes began to fill up.

"Alright, alright, calm down and don't get upset," Dave threw a tea towel at me and smirked. "If you think it will help we can try it. But we're not spending a fortune on it, you wanted these two terrors and now look; they're making you cry."

"I know but they make me smile so much too and I love them and their quirky ways, you love them too I know you do. It's just this one thing that's driving me crazy." I placed my hands on my temples as I said the word that described every walk with these two terriers.

We decided on a trainer; Mick, an ex RAF dog handler. He seemed pretty clued up over the phone especially compared to some of the chancers we'd spoken to.

He ran a charity rescuing problem dogs, trained them then rehomed them as model canine citizens. Without him these dogs would probably have ended up on death row, meaning this man could not only train dogs; he had a heart too.

Mick knocked on the door of our little townhouse. When I opened the door standing there was a well built, middle aged man with a crew cut. Looking at him you could understand why dogs sat up and took notice. He gave off a 'calm yet no nonsense' attitude. You could call it the infamous 'Calm Assertive Energy'.

"Well I see you weren't exaggerating about the barking." He wasn't appalled or judgemental, I got the impression though that he was thinking he had his work cut out here. We sat and talked over the issues I was having walking the dogs and generally having any control over them.

"Well the main thing is gaining their respect and all other things will fall into place." As he told us what to do he made it sound so simple; it's just more difficult than it sounds when your dogs are going all Charles Bronson because someone's at the door.

In a nutshell Mick's methods were; dogs have their place, and if they step out of line then they get punished. It sounds harsh I know, and believe me it felt it too. It did insight the question though of whether it was because I thought of Ronnie and Tess as my babies, or whether it actually was harsh.

Mick recommended a book to me about my little Jacks' ancestor; the wolf. As I lay in bed reading about these beautiful creatures something seemed to awaken inside me. I was excited, and soaked in the knowledge like a sponge. Apparently in the wild, wolves, the closest relatives of our canine friends, take discipline very seriously. It is one of the main learning curves for pups. They start with a low growl to warn the behaviour is unacceptable; if this is ignored they persist with a growl with intermittent sharp barks. If the behaviour continues they lunge and pin the pup/wolf by the neck and hold them there until they display a calm energy. This all looks very dramatic if you see it, but the idea is not to hurt the pup or fellow wolf, just to put them in their place. And if you have ever seen a wolf you will know if they wanted to inflict injury it would be easy, but they are surprisingly gentle and controlled.

These behaviours are what Mick based his methods on, but no Dave and I didn't go around growling in public. Not that I didn't try it from time just to see; and it did actually work. I just couldn't do it as we passed other dogs, I mean; what would the owners think? His methods were more about your energy, body language, protecting your personal space and lead corrections. The results were undeniable. We were obviously speaking a language our dogs understood because the change in our dogs' behaviour was amazing; to the point that on a walk they walked behind us, yes behind.

The trouble was that after a couple of weeks we'd slip back into baby voices, cuddles on the sofa and all the attention they demanded. Then they would slip back into pulling us down the road, play

15

fighting all over the house, barking at every noise and terrorising the neighbourhood.

Mick told us it really was just a patience game. If we stuck to the strict methods for a few months we could gradually add in privileges like cuddles on the sofa and playtime and probably have that plus complete control. But I just couldn't live without the closeness I'd shared with my dogs all this time, not even for a few months; not even for complete control.

I believe they call that 'a glutton for punishment.'

Needless to say Mick came back to our house many a time over the next couple of years and even became somebody I'm proud to call a friend. We'd go walks in the park; my terrors and I and his immaculately behaved wolf dog and collie and him. He never judged us (well not outwardly anyway) despite the fact we needed his help time and time again.

The dogs' behaviour did improve over the next couple of years, by no means to the extent we wanted but that's because we didn't do as we were told. But walks weren't quite so frustrating and draining, most days I actually enjoyed walking them. It's just as soon as I started to think, maybe I can cope with these dogs, I would take them a walk, meet ten dogs and be right back at square one crying in desperation again.

We tried other trainers, other methods. We made the dogs a sand pit in the garden to release their instinct to dig, we put them on a raw food diet, walked them more; but nothing worked. I began to accept that my two little dogs were who they were and that was that.

I think we all still have so much to learn about these creatures we call our best friends. How can they be our best friends when we don't even understand them? Don't get me wrong we love our dogs, but they are expected to simply fit in to our human lives. When that doesn't happen we shout at them, hit them with a newspaper, shut them outside, and that's just the average family. I hold my hands up to having done all of the above at some point but I'm certainly not proud of it.

Imagine what life must be like for those dogs in the not so average family home. Where the newspaper becomes a crowbar, shouting becomes slurring, unpredictable aggression and being shut outside means being wet, cold and lonely for hours on end. When I see these cruelty cases I cry inside and out and I'm ashamed to be a part of the human race. It can be so egotistical and arrogant; mistakenly thinking it's superior to all other species on this planet. Sure, we can build aeroplanes, make computers, fancy mobile phones, expensive cars. But we are also too stupid and greedy to realise we are killing our planet. Not only with fuels and the global warming crisis but we are literally killing each other.

We could, and should, learn a lot from our canine friends. They don't need gadgets and expensive clothes, nor do they care if they sleep in a one bedroom flat or a mansion. They don't bare grudges or long for what they haven't got. They don't think about yesterday or worry about tomorrow. As long as they are fed, walked, warm, dry and loved; they are happy. If we could think like dogs, just a little more, I think we would all find some peace. Mine had certainly taught me to appreciate the smaller things and to smile more and despite being a complete nightmare at times; the pair of them had made me happier just by being there next to me.

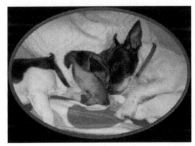

Chapter 5

A New Path

Everything I'd learnt about dog behaviour had opened a new chapter in my life with regard to what interested me. Basically if it wasn't dog related I was bored.

Consequently working with children no longer challenged me in the way I wanted; I yearned to work with dogs.

After scouring the internet, any job I was interested in required a Science GCSE qualification, (the only one I failed; what a Bunsen burner and dissecting a frog has to do with dog behaviour I don't know) or experience with dogs. I certainly didn't fancy sitting through Science lectures again so I started ringing boarding kennels from the yellow pages. I thought if I could get some experience caring for dogs then it could open other doors for me. It must have taken 6 months but after asking for a job for the millionth time someone actually said yes, yes we have a job vacancy. I had an interview at a kennels.

On the morning of the interview I was so excited; I'd waited for this opportunity for so long. But I had a dilemma. Do you dress to impress, as I'd had to do with every other job interview I'd ever attended, or do you dress in the suitable attire; jeans, wellies and a jumper? I changed and changed again but decided on the wellies with the hope that it was the right choice.

"Good luck babe," Dave gave me a kiss as he got into his work van and I got into my battered little Corsa." All of the training and information had sent Dave in the opposite direction to me with regards to dogs. He loved ours but that's as far as it went. So ultimately I think I bored him senseless with my rants about dog behaviour, dog welfare, dogs, dogs, dogs. He also was a little baffled by the idea of me working with dogs when I had worked hard to obtain a degree in Children's services. But what can I say; I changed my mind.

As I drove down the country lanes, looking out the window, I smiled. Yes. This is more like it.

Upon entering the tiny reception I was greeted by a middle aged woman with short blond hair (and lots of barking). She was a large lady and the moment she started talking, she scared the living daylights out of me.

"So why do you want to work in my Kennels Emma?" It crossed my mind then that she had brought me here just to tell me there was no chance in hell I could work in 'her' kennels.

"Err, well, because I love dogs and really want to work with them." I just about managed to stutter out this infantile sentence. Inside I shamefully shook my head at myself.

"Well lots of people love animals it doesn't mean you can work in a kennels, it's not all cuddles with the dogs you know. We have to work hard and what are you seven stone wet through?"

I was speechless, and fuming. How god damn rude! Ok so I was seven and a half stone, but it didn't mean just because I wasn't the size of her I couldn't do the job. I instantly disliked this woman, but it had taken me a long time to get this close to starting my career with dogs and I wasn't about to let this woman on a power trip get in my way.

"Yes I weigh about seven stone and I'm aware there is a lot of cleaning involved, as well as feeding and exercising but I'm prepared to give this everything I have and I know I can do it."

Her face was the picture of contemplation. Looking at me like a piece of meat. I could feel my temper rise and I knew that this woman and I would be coming to blows sooner or later.

"Ok well we'll see this morning, now let's have a look what you've got on." She got up and walked around to my side of the desk and looked at my clothes and feet. I waited on tender hooks, praying the jeans and wellies were the right choice.

"Ok, good, let's go through to block C and Nicola will get you started." I breathed a sigh of relief and followed her large behind through the swing door. On the left, on the way past, were blocks A and B. I had a quick glance through the door and the very sight made my tummy flutter with excitement.

As we went through to block C I took in the scene. We had walked into a long corridor; on the left was a row of kennels with hatches into outdoor runs. The kennels were all empty but with torn newspaper and the obvious mess you'd be expecting. I could hear the furry culprits from their outdoor runs.

The boss turned to me and said; "Good luck, I'll come and see you when you have finished." As she left I thought my god, this is a lot of kennels. Nicola; I'd say she was early twenties like me, with mousy brown hair scraped back into a ponytail. She took me through the process for cleaning the kennels and letting the dogs in and out. I asked her how long is usually takes and she replied ,"Oh about an hour to do the inside and a half hour to do the outside then feeding so you should be done around half ten."

Well I worked my little seven stone bum off and cleaned those kennels as well as I'd clean my house. I was careful to be kind to the dogs but not spend too much time with them until everyone had a clean kennel. The boss came back in around 10:30; I still hadn't finished the inside. Yet apparently I passed the test because she seemed very impressed and full from eating her words. She offered me the job. Hours were 8-12 and 4-7 five days a week. She mentioned one day I would be required to stay all day but that I could bring Ronnie and Tess with me.

So a few days later I started my first day complete with uniform. A navy blue polo shirt and fleece with the kennel name on. I felt so proud wearing it. I loved popping into the food shop on the way home seeing people looking and thinking to myself; yes, yes I'm one of those doggy people and proud of it.

The days turned into weeks and I got into the swing of things at the kennels and did my job well. Though I have to say I really thought there would be more time to actually spend with the dogs. By the time I had cleaned my block, seen to the cats and done all the feeds it was usually time to go home for lunch. Then when we returned at 4 o clock the tasks were feeding, let outs and more cleaning as most of the time the dogs had been cooped up since half 11 when we left. Oh and then there was feeding and cleaning the chickens. Yes chickens at a kennels; with dogs. Everyone else would probably realise that wasn't a very good idea but apparently not the boss. Most of the chickens were in an opposite enclosure, with a stream, a grassy area, trees and their coup. It truly was a lovely place for a group of rescued battery hens to live, just a dangerous one. Wendy, however, was special. The other chickens had cast her out, so she lived up at the kennels in her own coup, which was right next to one of the dogs' exercise areas (seriously). She was allowed to roam freely around the place and was more like a little dog than a chicken. The kennels also had their own cat that had strayed upon them and never left. You may think the cat would have attacked Wendy, the truth is she tried. But every time good old Wendy chased her off pecking her beak and flapping her wings. Yes, Wendy was definitely special.

Chapter 6

Sad dog days.

Part of the kennels was a dog grooming room, so we had to lend hands to that side of things with the little spare time we did get. Consequently the dogs barely had any attention. The only time they got to leave the boredom of their kennel was the two ten minute let outs they had in a whole day. Walking up and down my block to check everyone had water was so difficult for me. I'd see expectant faces with sad eyes and just want to climb in their kennel and shower them with love and cuddles. And sometimes I did, but it was not without reprimand. According to the boss there is plenty of cleaning to be done if I have finished the kennels; cuddling dogs was 'a waste of time'.

This really wasn't how I imagined it would be. It was as though the emotional needs of the dogs didn't matter as long as they were clean and fed. Those two things are the most important granted, but dogs needs expand much further than that don't they? They need exercise, a damn site more than two trips round the garden area. And the vast majority of these dogs were used to being part of a family, a pack. In these kennels they were isolated. So they were confused, lonely, and feeling abandoned. And I was told giving them a cuddle was a waste of time. To say I was angry about this would be an understatement. I have never been one to colour between the lines, so used to grab five minutes with the neediest dogs whenever I could...

...Toby was a Border Collie, black and white. Border Collies are renowned for their bond with their masters, it is in their DNA to work together with their handlers and they love to do it. So that probably explains why when Carly, the kennel supervisor, brought Toby through to my block he looked terrified. From the moment he stepped into that kennel it was as though he was sitting on a bed of glass. He was so on edge, so anxious, so lost. Toby was so scared that if you came too close he bared his teeth, held his ears flat to his head and growled. Ok, I thought to myself, this one's going to be tricky. But I was going to help him anyway I could. I wasn't about to just leave him there alone to suffer while I cleaned the windows; which is what would have earned me brownie points. Lucky I wasn't after those; I was here for the dogs not the manager's position.

So I began by sitting the other side of the kennel door, sideways. I'd recently learnt the way most of us approach dogs, especially scared ones, is wrong. Going towards a dog head on and smiling, says to a dog that you are a threat who is baring their teeth. Not the message I wanted to send poor old Toby. Sitting sideways let him know I was here but I wasn't demanding anything from him. I would just sit there for a few moments at a time speaking softly to him, for a couple of days, until the point came I decided it was safe to go in. Toby wasn't eating a thing and he'd been with us for 2 days. I slowly slid the metal lock open, walked through the gate and closed it behind me. I sat sideways to Toby as we had practised together and talked to him.

After a few minutes I picked up his food bowl and took out a couple of pieces of kibble. I extended my hand with the treats in towards Toby, but stopped a long way from his face. I desperately wanted to make this dog feel better but I didn't want to lose a hand. I left my hand there for what seemed like an age. Especially seeing as I wasn't looking at Toby, but eventually I felt a cold wet nose sniffing the biscuits, then a warm tongue scooped up the food and started crunching. I screamed 'yes' inside. It felt absolutely incredible that this dog had trusted me enough to take food from my hand. I kept on handing a few biscuits at a time to him and soon he had eaten half of the contents of his bowl. I was so pleased I had helped him, just a little, even if it was only to have a full tummy. I desperately wanted to fluff his ears and kiss his head but Toby wasn't there yet, I had to earn more of his trust for that.

"Emma!" Carly, the second in command to the wicked witch was calling. I slowly stood up, left Toby's kennel and walked through to reception.

"Hi, guess what, I just got Toby to eat some food" I said proud as punch. "Well have you cleaned everywhere else?" Carly wasn't impressed.

"Yes everyone is cleaned and fed," I sighed with disappointment and anger. What was wrong with these people?

"Well the boss wants you to go and do her dogs," Carly barely looked up from her paperwork. I thought 'oh great'. I loved the boss' dogs but resented the fact that I was meant to be here for the kennel dogs but spent half an hour of my valuable time throwing a ball in a field for dogs that were at home; their owner just couldn't be bothered to do it herself.

So poor old Toby would have to wait another day, as by the time I had done the boss' dogs, got the chickens in and checked on everyone it would be time to go home.

It was around my third week, when I came in after my day off and found Sophie in my kennel block. She was beautiful; a Golden Retriever pup about six months old. I presumed puppies would be allowed a little more attention than the adult dogs, but no this baby was still expected to cope with her first stay in kennels with no attention or cuddles. I did my usual secret cuddle stops with her until I was switched blocks around the second day into Sophie's stay. I didn't know if this was due to my disobedience of the rules but I expect it was.

Block C; the block I was in before being moved, was for the smaller and more frightened dogs. So I felt like a mother separated from her baby; knowing no-one else would look after those dogs like I did. After completing my duties in block B I would go and check on them. A young girl was taking care of them and to be honest I really didn't know what she was doing working in kennels. Her name was Lucy and she had little to no compassion for the dogs and everything was a joke. To be fair she was just a typical teenager, but it wasn't good enough.

Sophie; being a puppy, struggled to hold herself in between the 8 o clock and 4 o clock let outs. It's unbelievable; I was bewildered that nobody else thought this was disgusting even for the adult dogs. So whenever I went to check on Sophie she was usually sitting in her own wee or worse. Now I had never been the type of person to hold back when it came to reprimanding those I considered to be incompetent when animals were involved. In fact it was like a volcano eruption inside me.

"Lucy!" I called around the kennels looking for her after the sixth time I had found poor Sophie like this. I found her messing around in reception chatting like she had all the time in the world.

"What?" she answered in true teenage fashion. I told her to come with me and showed her Sophie's kennel.

"Oh Sophie you bad dog not again!" Lucy looked at me then said, "Why can't you do it anyway?" Let's just say I had to take a very deep breath. Lucy and I exchanged words and she sorted the kennel out but Sophie was stinking and I was worried about her getting sores, so I went to see the boss to get permission to bath her. Then I remembered I was meant to go through Carly; the only person I'd ever met who was literally dead inside when it came to dogs. Seriously what were these people doing there? Being a kennel maid is hardly a job you do unless you are besotted with dogs.

Carly was where she always was, sitting on reception playing with her diary.

"Hi, Sophie is covered in wee again; I'm going to give her a bath before I go home is that ok?"

"Well she's due to go home the day after tomorrow so she will need a bath the morning she goes anyway, so she will be fine for a couple of days." Carly barely looked up from her desk. I stressed she was quite soiled and I was concerned about her skin, but to no avail. In fact Carly didn't take too kindly to me questioning her authority at all.

I was fuming. I went out the back for a cigarette. I sat on the wooden bench and battled with my conscience and the fact that I had only been there a few weeks; I didn't want to end up being sacked. By the time I took the last drag on my cigarette I already knew Sophie was more important than being told off.

I stormed back into Carly,

"Look I'm going to bath Sophie, if the water and shampoo is that valuable take it out of my salary. I'm going to do it now before lunch. I'm on my own time and there's no-one in the grooming room so there's really no problem, is there?" As the words left my mouth I couldn't believe I was saying them to the second in command. Carly's face was a picture of disbelief and fury.

"Fine, but hurry up". She spat the words at me. Well that was that; Carly and I would never be friends. But as I bathed Sophie her big brown eyes looked into mine, she licked my cheek, and it was all worth it.

Chapter 7

Cabin Dogs.

Summer was in full flow; well the three weeks of summer we get here in England. This apparently was a boarding kennels' busiest time. Everyone was boarding those planes to paradise at once. This resulted in a lot of dogs coming through our doors for their 'holidays', their owners words not mine. If only they had known.

I arrived at work one day and started the daily routine in my block until Carly came in. "Emma I need you and Lucy to go and do the cabin and caravan dogs, Lucy will show you what to do." I was confused to say the least; I thought I'd had the tour when I started.

Lucy and I trekked down the country lane to the boss' house. As we walked through the back garden gate I saw the old porter cabin I had noticed when coming to throw those endless balls for her dogs. There was also a caravan that had seen better days. Then I heard barking.

"No way, in there?" I turned to Lucy in disbelief. We climbed three rusty metal steps into the cabin and inside were four tiny cages barely big enough for a rabbit. There was a dog in each with a bed, two pieces of soiled newspaper and a water bowl. My god. I thought things couldn't get any worse but they just had.

"We have to take them a little walk, just a few yards down the lane until they have done their business then we put them back in once we have cleaned it," Lucy said and began the chores as if this was nothing. I pulled myself together quickly; perhaps this is how things are done in all kennels. What did I know this was only my first job with dogs? Well I knew one thing. If this was my dog I'd be livid.

So to sum it up these poor dogs got five minutes down the lane at 8 o clock, then stared at four, very small, walls until 4 o clock when they got another five minutes and then that was it until morning. It made me heart ache leaving them in there and I'd go home and rehearse my attack on the boss. Something along the lines of 'if you think that's good animal welfare there is something seriously wrong with you.' The worst part was that the owners had no idea their beloved dog was in there. When they came to collect them we were made to bring them the back way in as though they had come from the kennels. On top of that dogs were put in the two caravans also in the gardens, which was fine when the weather was cooler. But they were put in there when the kennels were booked up; in the summer months. It was like a foreign country in those caravans.

That night I told Dave all about it.

"Are you ok, I mean all this with the staff, are you feeling ok?" Dave said. I knew he was referring to my earlier bout of depression. But surprisingly I didn't feel like that at all.

"No I'm not depressed babe don't think that. In fact in one respect I'm the happiest I've ever been in a job. The other staff and their downright stupidity irritate me yes. But walking into a room full of dogs every morning and making their stays that bit more bearable with my secret cuddles, makes me so happy." I looked into his eyes as he raised his eyebrows.

"What picking up poop and dealing with those morons every day?"

"Well obviously not those parts!" I smiled as I retaliated. "But just taking care of the dogs, just looking into their little eyes and showing them love just makes me feel..." I pursed my lips as I searched for the word "...fulfilled."

I knew from my reading, it had been proven that being around a dog does indeed make you happier. Stroking them reduces stress and depression due to increased serotonin levels in the brain. They can lower blood pressure and promote relaxation. Caring for dogs seems to fulfil a nurturing role within us. Plus there is just something magical about dogs, the connection they seem to have with people is indescribable.

Perhaps this is why the category of service dogs seems to be expanding by the day. For many years dogs have assisted the blind and deaf, but now assistance dogs help a range of people facing difficulties. These include; depression, the physically disabled, Autistic children and adults, children who have problems learning to read, people with epilepsy, they can sniff out cancer, they work with handlers in war zones, the list goes on and I'm sure will continue to grow. There is certainly more to dogs than most people give them credit for, and in my opinion they truly are angels on four legs.

Talking of people who don't give dogs the respect they deserve, kennel life continued to horrify me. Dogs shut in store rooms because kennels were full, (poor old Lily), dogs having to be dragged in the front door by their owners, dogs put in the cattery and cats stacked in crates in the caravans. One of these caravans turned out to be our staff room. This wouldn't have been terrible news, if you hadn't got to sit in it for four hours, in the heat of the summer. These were the days I had to stay all day as was mentioned in my interview. What wasn't mentioned was that I wouldn't be paid for this. Now I had established that I loved dogs but sitting in a caravan for four hours unpaid had naff all to do with a career with dogs.

This wasn't right was it? I thought to myself. I broached the subject with the other girls first, none of whom were happy about staying at work for four hours without pay either. So I suggested we all went to the boss to discuss it. Well, apparently I was working with a bunch of cowards. Still it didn't stop me. My mother brought me up to never let people take advantage of you; bosses, shop assistants, managers of food establishments; my role model has shown me how to deal with them all. So when the boss was next in reception I seized my opportunity.

"Hi boss, I wanted to talk to you about the days I'm required to stay all day. Firstly I'm very grateful you let me bring my dogs, I also love my job, I'm just not very happy with staying here for four hours unpaid." There, it was out now. Judging by the look on the boss' face she was mad; really mad.

"So you want me to pay you for sitting in the staff room?" This woman is from another planet if she thinks a caravan which hadn't been cleaned since its creation is a staff room.

"Well with all due respect, I do come and check on the dogs, feed and water the chickens and if anything happened during this time it would be my responsibility. Which I think does deserve some sort of wage," I seemed full of confidence but inside I was shaking like a leaf.

29

"I don't believe this." Her voice rose considerably. "If you don't stay then I can't leave the premises during 11:30 and 4:00, I will have no life I have been through a lot and I deserve to go out. You are the only person ever to have a problem with this do you know that?" She didn't get up from her seat; she didn't have to, her eyes burned into me like hot daggers. My heart was pounding and I felt the tears brewing. But I did not back down, I wouldn't.

"I'm sorry you have had a bad time but this is a business and it's not my responsibility to ensure you get to go out while I look after your business free of charge. And actually all of the girls are unhappy about staying for four hours unpaid but they are all too scared to tell you. So please don't single me out because I have the courage to come and talk to you rather than simply bad mouth you behind your back, boss." Now I was mad. And she was in disbelief.

"You are a liar, I will ask the girls if they have a problem and they will say no because they aren't selfish like you. And this is what it's like at all kennels so if you want to work with dogs you had better get used to working for free. Now get out before I say something I regret." Apparently she had reached her limit too. I stared at her for a moment, debating whether to tell her to stick her job. But if I left who would look after the dogs? I bit my tongue and stormed through the swing door to the kennels. I headed straight out for a cigarette before the rage could fly out of me.

One of the other girls came to sit on the bench with me. It was Sally.

"You ok?" She asked with a smile. Sally was lovely to me and the dogs. She had an air of understanding and compassion about her. Unfortunately one; She was a groomer, so after cleaning all her time had to go on that and two; she was a wimp, and didn't back me up.

Unbelievably things did blow over. We just didn't talk about it again. She continued being the boss and I continued being one of her gofers who worked for free.

When I wasn't at the kennels I was volunteering at a rescue centre, walking dogs; this is where I met Major. Major was a very large greyhound. He was all black apart from a white bib and grey muzzle. He had burns on his legs; he looked as though he had been used as an ash tray. Now walking rescue dogs sounds rewarding, and it was. But the pain in your arm when that dog is on the other end of a lead and hasn't seen outside in weeks is indescribable. It wasn't their fault they just needed a run, but I couldn't let them off or they would be gone. So clinging on for dear life it was. Apart from my Major, he plodded along next to me on a loose lead every time. He was so soft and gentle yet looking into his eyes you saw pain and fear. But with a kind stroke and scratch behind the ears I saw love and hope. I had fallen for this dog.

Unfortunately I had already told the head kennel maid all about Ronnie and Tess and their hatred of outsiders so I knew there wasn't a hope in hell of them letting me take Major home. I also wasn't sure my relationship with Dave could take another dog. Before he met me Dave wasn't all that into dogs. He had always had a family dog but could take them or leave them. But now he had two of his own. It probably would have been ok if Ronnie and Tess didn't push every button you had and make you want to jump off a bridge every time you took them a walk. I'm being unfair to them they are still adorable to me whatever they do; Dave just struggles a little more with forgiving and forgetting. Saying this both Tess and Ronnie have a lot more respect for Dave than they do for me. I'm the one who feeds them, walks them and lets them in the bed. And deep down I know Dave would never be without them either.

So there was only one thing for it, I had to find Major another home. Unfortunately the first person who came to mind was my boss. She was a lot of things but I do have to give her credit for the fact she rescued dogs nobody else wanted to take on. She had a deaf dog, a snappy dog, an out of control dog and old dogs. So I thought my old Major who was almost certainly not house trained would stand a chance there.

For a moment I thought twice about putting a dog I had fallen in love with into the care of this heartless woman. But the fact was she adored her own dogs; they had the run of the house and were looked after like royalty. It was other people's dogs she neglected.

It had been around a fortnight since our heated discussion and we were being civil to one another again. So when we were all helping to groom a very large Newfoundland with a terrible case of knots and tangles, I popped the question.

"I don't suppose you have room for one more dog in your house do you boss?"

"Absolutely not, I've got enough on my plate with the rebels I've got, why, who needs a home?" She seemed genuinely interested.

"Well I have been volunteering at the rescue kennels on my days off and have found Major. He's a greyhound about six or seven. He is just lovely but he has been there about six months now and one of the girls said he doesn't have long left." Unfortunately this particular rescue centre put dogs that were deemed as unadoptable to sleep. This classified as dogs who had been there six months with no interest. I was angry about this but they only had so many kennels and with dogs being abandoned everyday they did their best. It was just unfortunate for Major and his friends that their best wasn't enough.

"I hate that place," the boss said with a face scorned. "Have you tried ringing the Greyhound Rescue centre?" This was the most she had said to me since our argument.

"I doubt the kennels would let them take Major, I already asked the girl to ring me if his time was up because I would come and get him and try to find him a home myself. I couldn't believe it when she said I couldn't do that. I was told if I wasn't able to offer him a home myself and pay the money for him, apparently he is better off dead." I think the boss could hear the shared hatred for them in my voice and all of a sudden we had something in common.

"Well then you need to find someone who can have him." She did genuinely care about this dog she had never met, that softened my opinion of my boss, a little.

The next people on my list of potential owners for Major were my parents. They still had Bruno the Border Terrier puppy we kept about ten years ago but he was such a good old boy you barely knew he was there. They had a big house with a huge garden perfect for Major. The only problem being they had made it   very   clear during any of my earlier suggestions of a second dog that they weren't interested.

I speak to my parents every night; a habit I've had since moving out and years later still haven't managed to break. So every night for a long time I asked them to consider having Major. I pulled on their heart strings that he would die without them and begged them to go and meet him. Eventually, miraculously, they agreed to come to the kennels to take Major a walk. During the drive over Mum said her classic line of; "We are only having a look, we are not getting him today."

As soon as they brought Major out Dad took the lead and was smitten. Mum had Bruno, they had brought him just for a look too, and he seemed quite indifferent on the matter, more interested in weeing up trees and sniffing the ground. Dad on the other hand had fallen in love with my old boy. I didn't get too excited, knowing my dad. He is very, how shall we say, money orientated. If it cost money you had better jolly well need it otherwise it was a waste. A second dog certainly wasn't a necessity. The plan had never been to take Major that day, my parents were looking after our two for the next week as Dave and I were jetting off to Portugal. Dad, however, would not leave him in the kennels one more day, he had fallen in love with Major as quickly as I had and the rest, as they say, is history.

Major became Arthur and Arthur became part of our family. He gained a warm bed, food, a huge garden to run freely in and all the love and cuddles he wanted. Oh and his penguin, he loves his penguin.

Back at the kennels I was certainly back in good books for helping to rescue Arthur. My boss was so proud and I was shocked by how much I had wanted her approval. I suppose when I was bullied, by friends and enemies it left a few scars. I was lucky enough to have my family and some good friends to get me through those tough days. Now I have some amazing friends and that time is long behind me. The fact is that the feelings you experience never really leave you: Inadequacy, rejection, isolation, betrayal, the ache of hurt and the longing to be a part of what they have. Although you move on and life gets bigger and better, some things dwell under the surface; a scar hidden from view; stunting your soul's growth with whispering reminders. This is why having my boss' approval; her welcoming me into her fold, meant so much to me. Despite the fact I didn't want or need the blessing or approval of a self centred fool, it still felt good; it always does.

Chapter 8

A Bitter End...

It was the peak of summer and we were in the throes of a heat wave. It was my turn to stay all day; in the hot caravan. My dogs had to go into the porter cabin as there were no kennels. This piece of information was not revealed to me until I had arrived at work with my dogs, with no alternative but to leave them in there until I had finished the morning shift. So, not the best start to the day.

Sally had kindly decided to stay with me at work for the day so I at least had some company. Sally was a good person.

As soon as everyone else had gone home and I'd clocked out for the morning, I ran to go and get my dogs; they were very pleased to see me and be released from their dingy prison.

I took them up to the kennels and let them run off some steam in the exercise area. Wendy the chicken was strutting around the perimeter as usual and she had caught Tess' interest. Her tail was up, her ears were up, and she made an incessant whine at her frustration of the wire fence separating her from her pray.

I went and had lunch with Sally; we gossiped, watched daytime TV and had about as much fun as you can have in a mouldy, sweltering caravan. I then thought I'd bring Tess and Ronnie in with us for an hour before I put them away. I took their leads and opened the metal gate, as soon as they heard the clang of the metal on metal they came running, and Tess slipped past me. I wasn't too worried as I knew if Sally shouted her she would come, "Sal just shout...Tess!" I screamed her name but I wasn't fast enough. I had forgotten about Wendy, but Tess hadn't. As I'd been picking up Ronnie, Tess had made a beeline around the corner to where Wendy now screamed in panic and desperately flapped to escape Tess' jaws. Sally came running and I thrust Ronnie into her arms. In reflection a brave move, considering he was aggressive towards Sally as he was with everyone else, but it didn't even register then. I had one

34

priority; getting my killing machine away from that chicken. I grabbed Tess' jaws and tried to prise them open. I couldn't believe how locked her jaw was, I couldn't do it, all the while Wendy was squawking in pain. Adrenaline, panic and desperation rushed through my body. After what seemed like an age, but was probably only a few seconds, I managed to get Tess off her. I practically threw her in the caravan and ran back to Wendy where Sally was already looking for her. "She's gone I can't find her anywhere!" Sally had tears running down her face; Wendy had been her rescued chicken before she came to live here. I trekked up and down the bushed perimeter to the kennels property which is where Sally had seen her run to. We looked for almost an hour but at last I heard Sally shout;

"I've found her, she's alive!" I ran to her and was shocked to see Wendy looked ok, frightened but ok. Sally seemed so happy, "She's fine" she said as she gently moved her feathers around, but then we saw the blood. "Oh no" I whimpered.

"It's not too bad it's only a small wound I think she will be ok", Sally seemed so calm. "I don't know, I want to take her to a vet, you find a box and I'll get my car keys." The panic and fear still hadn't left me; this didn't feel like it was over.

I walked into the vet's examination room with Wendy in her little brown box. I had explained when I got there what had happened and they'd shown me straight in.

"These kinds of attacks don't usually end well for the chicken unfortunately." The vet looked at me apologetically and had that pitiful look in her eyes that vets only give at that certain time.

"No no you don't understand, the wound isn't that bad, look." I moved Wendy's feathers to reveal the small wound to the skin.

"Mmm, I see. Unfortunately a chicken's skin is not like ours and there are multiple layers which have been broken by the teeth of the dog, this will have been ripped further by her struggling to free herself. There's really not much I can do other than offer to euthanize her. I'm very sorry." The vet's pity overwhelmed me and the tears started, they really started.

"There must be some sort of operation you can do, surely?" I spluttered the words out through my sobs.

"We can but chickens don't fare well with anaesthetic and the results are likely that she would die on the operating table. I'm sorry; do you want me to call someone for you?" The vet passed me a box of tissues, noticeably unnerved by my reaction to a chicken being put down.

I wiped away the tears with the tissues, but then more filled my cheeks. "She's not my chicken; she's my boss', so you will need to call her to make that decision." I gave them the number but they suggested I ring. Fear and disinclination filled my throat as I waited for her to pick up.

"Hi, it's Emma. I'm at the vets with Wendy, I'm so sorry..." The tears took over and my words became one big wail and sob. I handed the phone to the vet, who after she put the phone down explained the boss was on her way. I had truly thought the intensity of my feelings could not get any worse; I was wrong.

The vet left me alone with Wendy while I waited for the boss. I gently stroked her feathers along her back; they were so soft. I leaned over and kissed her tiny head and whispered "I'm so sorry Wendy, I'm so sorry."

- - - - -

"What the hell has happened here, what dog got her?" The boss stormed in clearly fuming.

"It was Tess, I'm sorry." The tears were uncontrollable, partly invoked by fear and intimidation this time, but largely for the fact that I knew Wendy wouldn't be coming back to her patch outside the kennels. She wouldn't wonder in to reception for a cuddle, or follow us around as we worked outside. I had ruined her happy little life and devastated all those who loved her, including me.

"Get out, you can go, now!" The boss didn't even look at me, she was devastated and fuming.

I glanced back at Wendy sitting very still on the table, before I closed the door I heard the boss insist on the operation, so perhaps there was a chance.

- - - - -

Back at the kennels I had the heart wrenching and guilt stricken task of telling the other girls. We continued with the work for the afternoon filled with hope that Wendy would be ok.

Half way through cleaning my block Carly, the boss' golden girl, came in.

Before she even said I knew; "Wendy didn't make it. She died during the operation." I slid down the kennel wall into a heap of devastation all over again. I really thought she would pull through, despite the vet's words because Wendy was special. But Tess had just done too much damage.

I couldn't even look at my dog. I felt pure hatred alongside my love for her and it was just too much. After I finished my work, I made the short walk to my boss' house next door. I knocked on the door, my heart beating. I felt like I needed to apologise, however insignificant, or terrifying, it was.

She opened the door with red puffy eyes, as soon as she saw me her face hardened.

"I don't want to talk to you right now, I don't blame your dog I blame you!" With that she slammed the door in my face. Throughout the day the fear, the worry, the disbelief and the devastation had gathered, and with the door bang it all exploded.

- - - - -

"You can't just leave!" Sally tried to calm me down as the tears had taken over; I'd decided I had no option but to walk out of my job. "It will all blow over eventually, I mean I'm just as upset as the boss but I don't hate you, it just happened." Sal had a good heart, she must have hated me in some respect for what happened, but she never said it.

"I have to, I'm sorry but I don't think there's any coming back from this." I took a deep breath and eventually got the tears under control. The three cigarettes I had helped. As it grew dark I knew this day would be my last. I walked around the kennels and the sight of dogs and their big brown eyes brought back a lump in my throat. I made my way to Charlie's kennel. Charlie was a Blue Marl short haired Border collie. One of his ears stood up and the other one flopped over, he had gorgeous blue eyes and when you spoke to him his head cocked to the side. He was beautiful, and my favourite. He had been here three weeks as his owner was away on business. Every day after I'd finished the afternoon clean outs, I took Charlie onto the field behind the kennels. In that field he chased his little purple ball again and again and every time brought it back to my feet with his tongue hanging out and a face that said; 'just one more'.

I opened Charlie's kennel and climbed into his bed with him. I kissed his head and whispered; "its ok your dad is picking you up in two more sleeps."

He licked my cheek then jumped up, got his ball in his mouth and looked at me with a hopeful face. "Sorry boy, no more throws." My voice wobbled and a tear rolled down my cheek. I gave his head one last ruffle and left the block. With one last look over my shoulder, I saw his nose poking through the gate, and then and there; my heart broke.

On route to my car I knew I couldn't just leave without seeing her. So with trepidation I made my way back to the house. I knocked once more, my heart beating twice as fast as last time. I saw a shadow on the other side of the white door. "Who is it?"

"It's Emma."

"I told you I don't want to talk to you."

"I know but I'm going and I don't think I'm coming back so it's really now or never." I shouted through the door.

The key turned in the lock with a crunch and it opened a crack. "What do you mean you don't think you're coming back?"

"Can I come in and talk to you properly?" Well, I thought there's not really much to lose now. The boss opened the door and stood aside to let me in. I had never really been in the house before. She led me through to the kitchen and stood by the work counter. I looked around; on every available surface was a dirty pot or pan. The place was a mess. I looked at the woman stood before me and all my fear of her disappeared. She was just a lonely old woman who was angry at the world. Now that I was leaving she wasn't someone I needed to obey or be afraid of; she was just a woman.

"Well then let's hear it." The woman folded her arms and had a face scorned. I took a deep breath.

38

"I want to start with I'm so sorry for what happened to Wendy. Believe me you can't hate me more than I hate myself. I will have to live with this memory for the rest of my life. Every single animal is special to me and Wendy is...was, certainly no exception."

The conversation lasted a long time, and turned rather heated in places. She let out her anger on me and I told her a few home truths about how her kennels are run. She said I was good at my job and wanted me to stay, I said I had no choice now but to go.

What I hadn't told anyone was that I had already arranged an interview with another kennels two days ago. So this was fate. The day had taught me that fate can be cruel. If you are meant to be somewhere though, you will get there; the tribulations you face only lead you to your destiny.

- - - - -

I walked through my front door and hoped Dave was home. Ronnie and Tess ran in and found a comfy spot on the sofa. Oh to be a dog. Tess has probably forgotten all about the earlier devastation with no feeling of guilt or pain. Whereas I had a heavy feeling in my heart and I feared it would always be there.

"Hey you, how was work?" Dave came down the stairs and asked the question I'm sure he thought would have a simple answer.

He kissed me and caught the look in my eyes as they filled with tears yet again.

"What's happened?" His face frowned into the look of puzzlement. I fell into his arms and sobbed...and sobbed...and sobbed.

Chapter 9

Pond View

I was driving at 65 mph on route to Pond View Kennels via the bypass. Though I was surrounded by cars and the rolling tarmac; my mind was lost in my previous conversation with Mr Dale Fen.

"Hello, Pond View," a man with a broad Yorkshire accent answered the phone.

"Oh hi, my name's Emma. I work in a boarding kennels and wondered if I could just ask you a quick question?" The silence on the end of the phone was a fair reflection of my random phone call, accompanied by my bewildering question.

"Err, ok yeah what?" The man sounded mildly irritated. This was probably not due to the strange girl on the other end of the phone; but the fact that he was too intrigued to say no and hang up.

"My boss says I have to stay at work from eleven until four unpaid and she said this was the same in all kennels so I just wanted to check for myself." I blurted out the fact so fast I forgot to actually ask the question.

"I don't understand what you just said; you stay at work but don't get paid? Why?" The man sounded just as befuddled as I did.

"Basically what I wanted to know is; do you make your staff stay on the premises while you go out but refuse to pay them for it?" There was another long silence.

"No we don't do that. I don't understand what's going on where you work but that doesn't happen here. What was your name?"

"Emma. Thank you for that. I thought she was lying to me but I wanted to be sure." Thinking that would be the end of my conversation with the accommodating Yorkshire man, I got up ready to put the phone back on the receiver.

"Emma, I'm Dale. Emma, listen..." There was another long silence.

"Err, yes?" Now I was the confused one.

"Why don't you come down and see my place and I'll show you a proper kennels?"

I was completely taken by surprise. But looking down at the advert in the yellow pages, I was suddenly filled with curiosity and a confusing sense of optimism. "That would be lovely, I have a day off on Thursday, would then be ok?"

_ _ _ _ _

"Damn it!" In my daydreaming I had missed the turning for the kennels. I made a right at the roundabout and eventually turned into the kennel gates. As soon as I got out of the car I felt instantly at ease. I walked up the drive to find reception. Considering the close proximity to the road, the place was beautiful. On my left was a small pond, the whole perimeter was surrounded by tall green pine trees. On my right was a lovely bungalow enclosed by a walled garden. Adjacent to the bungalow were some gates, behind which there was a lot of barking; my favourite kind of noise.

Eventually I reached the end of the drive and in front of me was a small block of kennels and an exercise area. In the exercise area were four dogs; the sight of which filled me with butterflies and excitement. Despite longing to continue forwards for dog cuddles I turned right into reception.

Upon opening the white PVC door I was greeted by two women. Both were sitting at a worktop on tall stool chairs, they were nursing a cup of tea and looked like they had earned it.

"Hello love you must be Emma." The older of the two women stood up. She had short black hair and wore jeans, wellies and a black t-shirt. "I'm Denise, Dale will be here in a minute, can I get you a cuppa?" She radiated friendly yet competent warmth. She seemed wonderful.

"Yes that would be great, thank you."

"Take a seat, this is Lauren." She disappeared behind reception and through a door into what I presumed was the kitchen. I sat in the empty stool opposite the girl I now saw was about my age. She was blond and wore her hair in a ponytail. She also sported the kennel attire of jeans and wellies. Considering the awful experiences I'd had with kennel girls of late I felt surprisingly at ease with the one in front of me; who wasn't wearing a stitch of make up yet looked beautiful.

Denise returned with a hot cup of tea, and we gossiped like I had always been there. Then the kitchen door opened.

"Ay-up, don't be talking to these two lazy buggers!" A middle aged man dressed in a pair of very expensive looking wellies, some light blue jeans and a long sleeved check shirt, certainly made an entrance.

"You see what I have to put up with Emma, these two sat on their backsides while I'm working." The words were said in jest and he smiled at them. "Come on then, I'll show you my kennels. They're right kennels these, come through." His Yorkshire accent was so broad I only just made out what he said. I got up and followed him through the door, to the kitchen, which was modern and beautiful. "This is my feeding chart." Dale pointed up to a big white board with a grid of around 20 names with what they ate underneath. Under the worktops were white boxes marked; Bakers, Iams, Pedigree; the smell of dog food filled the large kitchen and it felt like home. There wasn't a dirty dog bowl in sight and tins were stacked high on the shelves.

"Wow. Now that is organised." I was impressed. "Back at the kennels from hell we were lucky if we had a scrap of paper saying what dogs ate what food."

"Yes well we are organised here, this kennels is run properly. Come through here then." He led me through the back door out too what looked like paradise. Immediately in front of me was a garden area, filled with small bushed plants, a picnic table and a path leading to the beautiful, beech wood cattery.

Behind the garden fence, which was around four feet high, was a huge green field with a stunning pond which was the size of half the field. Surrounding the pond were tall reeds and lily pads floated on the water. In the middle was an island tall with grass and plants. In the field rabbits hopped around and took shelter in the surrounding hedgerows. It was breath taking. And this was the dogs' view from their kennel. For a moment I couldn't speak.

"What do you think of my pond, nice isn't it?" Dale was clearly proud as punch of his patch of paradise.

"This is, amazing." That was all I could muster. I was in awe.

On the left were the metal gates to the kennels. The walkway to the kennels was accessed through two gates, one was shut before the other opened so that there was no chance of dogs escaping; I could have done with this system a couple of days ago.

Dale had the kennels along the left, and they were huge. So much space for the dogs; big expensive beds in the inside kennel which had a hatch to the run area. The run area, attached to the kennel, had green PVC walls and the kennels and run were housed under a PVC roof. The runs had a door leading to the walkway, on the other side of which was a big exercise area looking out to the big field and pond. So while stretching their legs the dogs could watch the rabbits running and the birds flying. It really was incredible.

"Dale these kennels are wonderful, just amazing. You should see where I have been working. The kennels are tiny the dogs are only let out into a boring grass area twice a day; this place puts it to shame. Truly, you should be really proud of what you have here." The words I managed to speak did not cover what I wanted to say; but there simply were no words. This place showed me beauty, love, happiness and hope. Walking up and down the kennels I didn't feel guilty, the dogs looked so content and very excited to see a new face; jumping up and down, wagging tails. There were no sad eyes and full food bowls, no whining and crying, just happy dogs. I smiled the biggest smile I had in a long time.

"What?" It hadn't escaped Dales notice.

"Nothing, I just love this place."

"Well how about seeing my dogs now?" My face must have spoken a thousand words; that or Dale was a mind reader.

"I breed dogs. I've got about 20; Labradors, Cockers and Shi-Tzus."

My smile grew even bigger. "I would love to see your dogs," I replied. I practically skipped over to the bungalow gates I saw earlier. Dale held the gate open for me and I walked through to see 3 more block of kennels in front of me. They were the same exceptional quality as the others, the difference being these blocks were left open; dogs ran around freely from their kennels to the exercise areas and in each block there were around 8 dogs, maybe less.

The dogs were beautiful. The cocker spaniels wagged their bottoms and leapt up to the fence to sniff me, the Labradors were black and golden; their big brown eyes looked into mine and I fell in love instantly.

Denise, who I'd guessed was Dale's wife, was busy hosing down in one of the exercise areas. She was surrounded by tiny fluffy dogs. I don't think I had seen a shi-tzu in the flesh before. They were the definition of cute. She greeted us with a smile and a wave and came out to stand with us. Dale searched for something in his pocket and brought out a small cardboard packet and a lighter. As he lit his cigarette I thought 'yes!' but then remembered I had left mine in the car.

"Do you smoke Emma?" Dale asked before taking a long drag on his Marlboro Red.

"I do but I left mine in the car, I didn't want to make a bad impression with them sticking out of my pocket," I smiled at the irony. I was grateful to be in the company of fellow smokers but gutted I was minus my cardboard packet. We smokers have become a somewhat small group; excluded from society due to negative government propaganda. I do find it quite contradictory however, that said government continue to reap the taxes from our 'disgusting' 'frowned upon' habit.

"Here you go" Dale held out his pack of cigs, I did not hesitate.

"Thank you, I'll go and get mine in a mo." I lit up and took a long drag of nicotine and social smoke.

"You're alright cock, we've got plenty. Let's go in for a cuppa, come on."

Inside the bungalow we sat at a large mahogany dining table. We were still smoking but were accompanied by a steamy cup of tea.

"So can I have a job then?" I just came out with it. Dale laughed at my candid spirit. I knew it was forthright but I wanted to work in this incredible place with every bone in my body. Dale looked across the table at Denise. "What do you think?"

"I don't know it's up to you," Denise replied "I didn't think we needed anyone at the moment that's all. You seem lovely Emma we just have Lauren already." Denise's eyes looked apologetic yet there was a hint of hesitance. She lit up a cigarette. "Saying that; I'd love an extra pair of hands but it's up to Mr Fen over there." Denise's glance turned from me to Dale and there was a long silence. I was beginning to get used to these. Dale pursed his lips in deep contemplation.

"Right," he stated. "Well it will only be 20 hours, and this is so you can go back home whenever Emma's here," he declared to Denise with accusation. "You can go shopping, whatever you want." He turned to me, "This one here is always moaning she never gets to go back up home to see family so she can now can't she? But it's only 20 hours I can't offer you full time or I'm eating into my profits. So it's up to you. Oh and you will have to have a trial first; see if you're any good."

An uncontrollable smile spread across my face. The excitement and adrenaline was racing through me. I can't believe I was coming to work here; at dog paradise. We arranged I'd come back in a couple of days. We spoke about my dogs and Dale sold me a kennel to put up in his field; provided I got the job of course. So my dogs would have their own little home while I was at work and I would always be close by to check on them; perfect. This felt like fate, I knew this was going to be my dream job.

Chapter 10

Trial and error.

I arrived 20 minutes early for my trail; which was to take place in the cattery. Apparently this was Denise's domain as Dale was not what you'd call a cat person.

Denise led me into the cattery; which compared to the last one I worked in was heaven. We walked into a small kitchen which housed the food, bowls, sink, bedding, trays, litter and a big feeding chart.

This led to the cattery. A long isle of what I can only describe as luxury log cabins for the cats. The sleeping compartment was up a ladder with a cat flap and a door. They had heat pads under their beds and a run area for their tray and toys. They also all had high ledges in the runs so they could watch out of the windows.

These cats were so lucky. As I stood in this wonderful place, I thought of the poor cats that would be in crates, in a dark caravan, back at the kennels from hell.

Denise took me through the routine and I was taken aback by how much she cared about the cats; their cleanliness, their comfort, their eating, everything. I had finally met someone who shared my thoughts and passion for animals. So I did exactly what she had asked of me and when I had finished I was called over to the house.

As I walked over my heart pounded; I really wanted this. I just hoped I'd done enough.

Sat at the big dining table with a cup of tea and a cigarette, once again, I felt like I was at home. I didn't want this to end.

"So then Emma, Denise said you did alright in the cattery, but I should think so it took you long enough," Dale said with a smile.

"Well quality before quantity Dale" I smiled back with my candid attitude once again. Denise laughed and called from the kitchen; "too right Emma."

"Well next time quality and quantity please. You can start on Monday and I'll show you how to do the kennels."

My uncontrollable smile was back. "That sounds great, thank you. I'll be the best worker you've ever had; just need a little training and I'll be as good as you." My cheeky smile greeted his 'no-one's as good as me' eyebrows.

- - - - -

So life at Pond View began. It must have been my first week as I recall being completely and utterly mortified. I was in charge of the small dog's block and Lauren was in charge of the big dogs. One of my little dogs was in season; I'd been cuddling her for a while when Lauren shouted from reception.

"Em, can you let Diesel out for me? I've just got to pop over to Dale's dogs to find him." I shouted sure and made my way up to the next block.

Standing outside Diesel's kennel the only thought running through my head was 'my God you are huge, and playful, and huge.' I pulled myself together opened his kennel and led him in to the exercise area. Diesel jumped up at me and it felt as though I'd been hit by a bus. He was only playing and wanting a cuddle; until he smelt my t shirt; the t shirt that my little in season bitch had been snuggling into moments before. He began to sniff me frantically, clearly excited at the prospect of a mate. What Diesel didn't seem to grasp was that I was not it. Diesel became crazed at the smell of my top and took his two front paws and clung on to my hips and began thrusting madly. This would have been little more than embarrassing if not for the fact his claws sunk into my flesh with all his body weight. "Diesel, off, Diesel!" I desperately tried to prise his claws from my hips; the problem I had was I needed to back up, turn around, open the exercise area and get out without diesel getting through the door with me. Every time I got his claws off and tried to turn round Diesel would clamp back onto me. I must have tried this for about five minutes before the pain from his claws became too much.

"Help! Somebody help!" I screamed at the top of my lungs. Dale flew down the kennels a few minutes later, his face terrified I had been attacked. When he saw diesel humping away his face broke into laughter.

"What the hell's going on here?" He came in freed me from the clutches of the horniest dog I have ever met.

"My god Dale look what he did to me," I examined the red and purple bruises on my hips.

"He must have taken a fancy to you he's not done that before." I confessed to my silly mistake and he laughed.

"Well you've learnt that lesson I trust? I sheepishly nodded my head; still mortified at the embarrassment. I thought to myself; 'yes, don't cuddle in season bitches and then visit an intact male. To him you will smell like his one true love, he will not care, or even notice that you have two legs instead of four. The heart wants what the heart wants.'

Those first few weeks were certainly a learning curve. Dale was very particular about how things should be done and when they should be done; rightly so too. It just took a little getting used to, well the main man himself did.

Dale had moved here from Yorkshire to set up these kennels; though I got the impression it was more Denise's dream than his. He had owned a timber yard, a pub and from what I could tell had worked extremely hard for what he now had; a beautiful plot of land and a successful business. Though he was clearly quite comfortable when it came to money these days, he had not lost the value of it. It's true what they say about people with money; they are the ones most reluctant to spend it. This was Dale most of the time, but every now and again he would make a generous gesture that gave people a glimpse of the heart he tried to keep hidden away.

He was very proud of his pond; the one the lucky dogs viewed from the exercise areas. If you couldn't find him he was feeding the fish, sorting out the water pumps or letting his dogs out for a swim in the water. It feels derogatory calling it a pond; seeing as it was the size of a small lake. Then there was the lawn mowing. As you can imagine there was quite a bit of grass on the kennel grounds and Dale spent around 50% of his week on a ride on mower; which he loved. Dale was always in a good mood on grass cutting day. Dale and his moods dictated most of our days. When he was in a good mood we would all sit and drink tea, smoke and put the world to rights. We would laugh, joke and all work well together. I also soon realised that at times Mr Dale Fen should be completely ignored.

One such morning the smell of dog excrement filled the garden. The kennels were operated on a pump system, with regards to waste. On more than one occasion these pumps decided to cease working; which led to Dale spending most of the morning with his hands down a hole full to the brim with faeces. This, as you can imagine, put Dale in one hell of a mood. On these days everything Lauren, Denise and I did was wrong and his mouth rarely uttered a word that wasn't a curse. I soon learnt to either ignore Mr Fen on these mornings, or answer him back with a few curse words of my own and tell him to lighten up.

You may think this would get me the sack, but working here was like no other job I'd had. It really was like working for family and everyday getting out of bed to put on wellies was easy. I never got that dreaded feeling of going to work; I loved being there and even went in for a cup of tea on my days off. My wise Grandma once said to me; "you must love your job because you are at work more than you are at home; if you're happy at work you're happy in life."

I felt as though I'd finally found where I belonged.

Chapter 11

Happy dog days.

I had been dreading working with another young girl as my previous experiences had been either intimidating or frustrating. Lauren, as it turned out; was wonderful. She had the same attitude to dogs as I did and took the very best care of them during their stays at Pond View. She happened to be only two years younger than me and we looked after each other. I find it a confirmation of fate that we meet people we never would have met; had we not taken that opportunity that presented itself. It has been my experience that these people emerge to be incredible influences in our lives and the very best friends.

It was a beautiful summer's day and Lauren and I decided to take Chad; a very large and unpredictable Japanese Akita, out onto the field for a walk and a sniff. Chad was beautiful. He had cream short fuzzy fur with black markings around his neck and face. You could call Chad a little misunderstood; but some would call him terrifying. It was mainly men Chad had an issue with; he most certainly did not approve of Dale anywhere near his kennel but just about tolerated Lauren and I seeing as we were of the female kind. Hence why we were taking Chad out for a little relaxing walk, try to ease his obviously tense attitude to kennels.

I entered the enclosure and clipped a lead to Chad's collar.

"Em, are you sure an extendable lead is a good idea? He is really strong you know, perhaps just a short lead would be better." Lauren was visibly concerned about my choice of lead for the huge and powerful Chad; I on the other hand seemed to be oblivious.

"Oh it will be fine, I want him to be able to have a good run about and sniff all the smells." So out we went on to the big field which was another part of these beautiful kennels. This field was behind the kennel blocks opposite to the field with the pond. Lauren closed the gate behind us and I pressed the button on the lead which released the extendable long lead.

Chad sniffed happily away while Lauren and I walked and gossiped about our men. You could hear the birds chirping and feel the soft grass underfoot. This went well for about ten minutes. We turned around to walk back and Chad began to run; I mean really run. I braced myself and held on to the lead handle with all I had. I knew what was going to happen; the lead was going to run out really soon. When this happened Chad would either fly backwards possibly damaging his neck, or; "CLACK!!!" It all happened so fast. The lead clicked then I flew forwards with such a force I landed face first into the grass and the lead flew out of my hands. From my place on the floor I heard Lauren running over, laughing uncontrollably. "Oh my god, are you ok?" She was concerned in between understandable hysterics. "Yeah I'm fine; get Chad before he gets over that fence!" The fencing around the field was tall enough to contain most dogs; but Chad was not stopped by many things. He'd taken the naive seven stone girl on the end of his lead down like a playing card in the wind. Lauren rained Chad in and all was safe. The relief waved through me and I stood up. "Ouch!" Now the adrenaline had worn off the pain throbbed in my wrist; apparently I'd landed on my face and my wrist. "I hate to say I told you so but....." Lauren's face was trying so hard not to burst once again into laughter.

"Yeah ok lesson learnt smart ass!" I playfully pushed her and slowly broke into a fit of laughter myself. This of course started Lauren off again. "Seriously good luck explaining that to Dale" she nodded at my wrist; which I was rubbing. "He will never let you live that down; he's still on the Diesel incident and that was two months ago!" Well; another lesson learnt.

I had been at the kennels for a few months now and while my job was to care for the boarding dogs; whenever I had a spare hour I would go over to the breeding kennels for puppy cuddles.

The puppies and caring for the puppy mummy was Denise's job. What can I say about Denise? Well for a start she was like me, just in twenty years time. She talked to the dogs like they were her babies, she cooked them chicken when they wouldn't eat, named each and every puppy and shed a tear when they went to their new homes. She was always so kind to me too. We'd chat over a cup of tea on our breaks and she would always ask how the boarding dogs were. Denise, quite simply was; wonderful.

The sun was shining as I made my way over to the big wooden gate; behind which were the breeding dogs and their beautiful babies. I pushed on the gate but it didn't open. The top stuck sometimes so I took a deep breath and barged the gate with my shoulder; I flew through it this time, literally. I steadied myself and closed the gate behind me. When I turned around I saw Dale standing there with a huge smug grin on his face.

"Oh yeah saw that did you?" I playfully reprimanded his grin and walked over.

"Right you seeing as you're here you can help me worm these pups."

My tummy fluttered with excitement. This meant I could give each and every puppy a cuddle. This was a good day.

After all the puppies had been squirted in their mouths with sticky pink liquid to kill any retched worms in their tummies, it was run around time. I was sat on the grass surrounded by eight cocker spaniel puppies. They were about six weeks old and full of life. They bounced around rolling over and playing with their brothers and sisters.

Before coming here I don't think I had ever seen a cocker spaniel in the flesh. I had always been a terrier girl and although I loved all dogs I'd never even contemplated having any other dog. Looking at them then though it's safe to say I was sold on the cocker spaniel front. As they ran with their tongues hanging out and their long ears flapping it was impossible not to fall in love. One puppy came over to me and began chewing on my boot.

"Well you're going to be a handful aren't you?" I picked up the tan and white puppy and held it in front of my face; where it began licking my nose. As I placed the pup back down I looked around and couldn't believe I was here; that this was my job. I felt like the luckiest girl in the world.

Denise popped her head out of the back door to the bungalow as the pups ran around in the garden.

"Oh hi love, you having cuddles my beautiful babies? I see you met my little Annie cupcake," she said with a big smile on her face. Annie ran off to join her littermates.

"Yeah, they are just gorgeous Denise." I got up as now she was back I could get back to Lauren and the boarding dogs. I had a quick chat with her then made my way over to the kennel kitchen; it was feeding time and 20 dogs wanted their dinner.

Chapter 12

Megan.

When I was a little girl I loved all the dog films. The fairytale princess stories never really appealed to me; despite being what most people would call a 'girly girl'. When I look back there were so many; 101 Dalmatians, Lady and the Tramp, BINGO, Lassie and not forgetting my favourite; Homeward Bound.

These films paint a picture of an unbreakable friendship; a love like no other and a magical connection between dog and owner. I had watched these films and dreamed one day I too would find my special dog; the one who would know when to cuddle me when I was sad, the one who would play when I needed to laugh, the one who would rescue me; the one.

My parents are realists, not dreamers like me. So as soon as I was deemed old enough for the truth they hit me with it. These were just films. There is no magical dog that will rest its paw on your shoulder when you cry, no dog that will run all the way home from the kennels just to find you. There is no dog that will rescue you from a burning building, no dog who will wait for you to come home from school at the end of the garden; no dog.

My parents have always had a dog in their home, and they give them a wonderful life; but 'a dog is a dog'. So I don't know where this dog obsession started. I have always felt that dogs are equal to us not below us; that they have thoughts and feelings, that they are sacred, precious.

So they told me there was no such dog, and I doubted it myself for a little while; until Megan.

"Will you at least consider it?" Dave stared at the TV and completely ignored me. We had been 'having words' for over an hour. I had decided I desperately wanted to add a cocker spaniel puppy to our family. This had not gone down well.

"We already have two dogs which are enough of a nightmare as it is; train these two then I'll think about it."

"But Dave they are un-trainable! I have tried everything and got nowhere. I think we both have to respect the fact they are the way they are now, they're just true Jack Russells. I just want a dog I can walk off the lead, that I can take to the pet shop and round to my friends houses. A Cocker Spaniel is such a friendly dog she wouldn't be a problem. Please Dave, just think about it?" I displayed my best puppy dog eyes.

"I will THINK about coming up to the kennels to see the puppies but that's as far as it goes." He turned up the TV and that was the end of that conversation; for now.

Dave is the complete opposite of me in each and every way. I am small and skinny; he is tall with a manly build. I'm dog crazy; he likes cats. I'm vegetarian; he is a big meat lover. I believe in a God; he believes in the big bang.

Our discussions about the world always end up heated ones because one thing we do have in common is that we are always right. Despite our differences we seem to work. He keeps me grounded and I teach him to dream.

Dave hasn't had the easiest of lives; though he would never tell you that. In the face of this he went on to make a success of his life when he had the easier choice of a life on Welfare benefits before him. He worked from the age of sixteen and still works his fingers to the bone for all he has. This is actually another thing we have in common, not the hard life part; I had a wonderful childhood, the teens were difficult and naturally I hated my parents as they were ruining my life, but other than that things were good. I mean the working hard part. I started working at the age of fourteen in weekend jobs. I may not have come from a difficult background but I was by no means spoilt which I am eternally grateful for. I was taught if I wanted money I had to earn it.

So I suppose Dave and I are compatible in some ways and complete opposites in others; just the right amount of conflict to find out who you are and enough harmony to feel at peace with one another. But at times like these I wished he was as crazy about dogs as I was.

The weeks passed and eventually he came to work with me one day to see the puppies. I had a favourite of course; little Annie Teacup. Denise had aptly named the lemon roan pup as she was the tiniest of the litter.

Dave bent over the puppy run and stroked the bundles of fur and wiggles. "So what do you think can I have little Annie?" I picked her up and together we gave him the puppy dog eyes.

Dave laughed, "Em that's not going to work, I really don't think we need another dog. I said I'd come to see them and I know you were hoping I'd see them and change my mind but I haven't."

My heart sank, but then my blood boiled. When I said I wasn't spoilt Dave would have disagreed. I definitely don't think the world owes me anything and I work hard for what I have; but if there is something I have set my heart on, I usually get it; one way or another. This time however it seemed that was not going to be the case. I did not take it well.

The days passed and Annie found her home, then I set my heart on Amber a chocolate spaniel pup, then she found her home.

Lauren and I were having our tea break one morning when Dale came to join us. He was accompanied by his customary cigarette.

"Morning Dale, what's up with your grumpy face? I began with our routine banter. Today however he was not in the bantering mood.

"Ah we've had some pups die and the mum's so stressed she's pulling her hair out. She's only got one pup left poor bugger." Dale rubbed his hand over his head in despair. "Denise is giving her lots of attention like, she's getting fresh chicken for her dinner, dog's eating better than me," Dale smiled but it quickly faded and his anguish returned.

"Oh Dale I'm so sorry, how come this happened? Which of your dogs is it?" Anguish had spread from his face to mine, this was devastating.

"Our Sally, I don't know cock, think she just had too many, ten pups is too many they were too small." Dale took a long drag on his cigarette. Nine puppies, the thought hit me hard, poor Sally. Sally was a chocolate Cocker Spaniel. She had a collection of curly hair on top of her head which I called her perm. Sally was one of my favourites, what am I saying she was undisputedly my favourite. So this was devastating news.

"Can I go and see her?" As I asked Dale I knew the answer already.

"No cock it'll just stress her out more, leave her be with her pup. Denise is looking after her. You can see her in a few days if she improves."

Lauren and I were sad for the rest of the day; it had clearly devastated Dale and Denise too.

A few days later Dale took me over to see Sally and her remaining pup; who was doing well. It was the little piece of good news everyone needed, including Sally who was doing much better.

"Hey Sal" I couldn't help but smile when I saw her; I loved this girl. I bent down to stroke her curly top and she snuggled into me. Then I heard a squeak which didn't go unnoticed by her either. Sally went running over to the bed inside her kennel where a little brown head popped up and two paws rested on the rim of the bed. My heart almost burst with amazement. She was the most beautiful puppy I had ever seen. Dale must have seen my reaction as he came into the kennel, gently picked the puppy up to show me and said; "This is your pup then?"

From the moment I saw her I knew she was my girl. So after another few days of persistent pleading, Dave came to meet her. He had the same reaction as me; his face the picture of adoration. Soon after meeting her Dave caved and agreed I could have her. To say I was happy would be an understatement. Every spare minute I got I was over at the breeding kennels with Sally and the puppy. She was only four weeks old so I had a long wait until she was coming home with me. But she was worth every second and after seeing her no other puppy would do; she was the one.

Sally soon felt better too and the hair on her back was growing back nicely. She seemed to approve of me as a new mummy for her only baby. She never minded as I handled the pup and was usually more interested in sniffing my pockets for the treats I brought her.

Of course now Dave had agreed, I had two other family members to convince; Ronnie and Tess.

– – – – –

The time had come to name the new member of our family. Not too difficult you'd think? The trouble was she needed a special name; to be the only surviving puppy from a litter of ten she was obviously a special dog. After much deliberation I named her Megan. Her name has numerous meanings. The Welsh meaning is 'little Pearl'. In Greek the meaning of Megan is 'child of light' and in Anglo – Saxon Megan means 'strong'. I thought it was perfect for my beautiful, miraculous survivor.

Denise was understandably a little hesitant about homing Megan with a pair of dogs as complex as Ronnie and Tess but agreed I could give it a go. Dale on the other hand was quite relaxed about the whole thing:

"Ah they'll be 'right, you've just got to let them see her, take her over to the field and let them see her through the kennel to start with." So that's exactly what we did; Lauren and I. Every lunch break I'd go and collect Megan and we'd sit on the field with her and let her play. She loved Ronnie and Tess and didn't want to be anywhere but the other side of the kennel door licking their noses through the bars. Tess seemed to quite like this; Ronnie on the other hand was quite aloof to the whole matter. But we persisted and after a while dared to let them out to run around with her one at a time. Tess loved her and they played chase all around the field; I naturally had my heart in my mouth at these times but sometimes there's no option but to trust your dog and your judgement. Ronnie was tolerant of her persistent approaches and when he'd had enough would give her a low growl and she would trundle off to find Tessie.

I'll never forget the first time Megan made me laugh. She was playing on the other side of the field and I called her over. Her little head popped up and turned around - she paused for a second as if considering her options then tore towards us at full speed; her ears flapped in the wind and her tongue hung out the side of her mouth and she looked as though she was smiling. It was the most wonderful sight in the world and Lauren and I rolled around giggling as she ran into our arms. That was a good day.

Chapter 13

Home time.

After what seemed like the longest month if my life, I carried a nine week old Megan into the house. I put her onto the soft carpet – something she'd not seen before - she sniffed the floor like a bloodhound and found her way to the garden where she was in heaven exploring her new home.

Megan was my shadow right from that first day. If I went for a bath she would curl up on my dressing gown and wait for me. If I went outside for my cigarettes she would wait by the door until I walked back through it. When I settled down on the sofa for the evening Megan would be right there, often laying on my chest with her head in my neck, just like my Bruno used to do. Of course the larger she grew the less comfortable this became, I had to relocate her to cuddling into me instead. I'd lie on my side and Megan would sit in the curved shaped space by my tummy. She made that her spot.

Megan turned out to be just the dog I'd dreamed of; Ronnie and Tess weren't the cuddling type these days, they preferred play time and a good chew. Megan on the other hand couldn't get close enough to you; a medicine I willingly received.

Jack Russells certainly get old before their time and like their own space. I still love every hair on their body with all that I have, but I respect that they are who they are and have stopped trying to mould them into different dogs.

My life has, at times, been full of strife. Although you move on from these nightmares and continue with the journey of your life; parts of the nightmare haunt you forever. One such haunting for me is The Big Red Bus.

I'd met Dave while I was still at school, a few months before my sixteenth birthday. He lived in the city about 30 miles from me. So on a Friday I'd hitch a ride - from my little town to the city - on the school bus my friend caught. The driver really shouldn't have done this as it wasn't policy; but he was the type of man who broke the rules. One particular day my friend - who normally rode all the way to the city with me - was off school so for the second half of the journey it was just me and the driver. Now at this age I was the typical naive fifteen year old girl. I was also (I'm told) a very attractive fifteen year old girl. Despite the bullying I suffered at school I was still a very chatty and friendly person and as it was just the driver and me on the bus I felt rude not going to talk to him for the rest of our journey. Unfortunately this transpired to be one of the biggest mistakes of my life. After exchanging banter for a few minutes the driver pulled the bus over in an old country lane. Apparently being a friendly attractive schoolgirl, translated into being fair game for a man in his thirties. I won't go into details as I'm sure you get the picture of the scene that followed. Needless to say this was an unspeakable injustice, it did teach me invaluable lessons but this particular nightmare will always be with me.

It wasn't long after I'd brought Megan home, she must have been about eleven weeks old. I'd just been out for lunch with a friend and was travelling home in my car. I turned down a street and slowed to a crawl in a line of traffic. In front of me was a big red bus transporting schoolchildren home. I had to follow this bus for about

61

a mile. Just seeing it, although perhaps not the same bus; made my stomach knot. My mouth literally watered with nausea, my breathing accelerated. I pulled onto my drive and fumbled for my house key. I dropped them on the step outside my front door; they made the muffled ring of metal on concrete. I turned the key in the lock, went in and locked the door behind me. My heart was pumping; 'thud thud thud!' I made my way into the kitchen to let the dogs out. I had the usual mauling of joy from Ronnie and Tess who then ran outside for a wee. Megan on the other hand wouldn't go out. "Go on Megs out for a wee poppet" I tried to say with some normality. But she just came and sat at my feet, I bent down to her and she rested her front paws – very gently – on my knees. She looked into my eyes for a few seconds, nudged my cheek with her nose which made me smile, then she ran outside to join the others. Some people say dogs are stupid, oblivious, that they only care about food and balls; those people are wrong.

– – – – –

After a lot of growling, teeth bearing, sulking and shouting, correcting and training; our three dogs now cuddled up together and I could leave them in the same room while I went upstairs without fearing for Megan's life. Adding a dog to your pack is no easy task let that be said, but the gain in the end makes it all worth wile.

Chapter 14

The Big Dog

I'd been off work for a couple of weeks settling Megan in but was now busy rounding three dogs up at 7: 15 am on a Monday morning.

I pulled up and parked the car. Dale came out of reception with a face like thunder. I looked at the clock on my dashboard; 7:40 – five minutes early. So I'm not late at least.

"Morning Dale", I shouted from my car as I clambered out.

"Come on get them bloody dogs away and get to work we're busy and Lauren isn't here yet," he said as he stormed back into reception. Oh dear Lauren and I were in for a day of Dale's tantrums. I don't think men ever truly grow up out of their adolescent sulks and today was clearly going to be one of those days.

Lauren and I reacted to Dales moods very differently. Lauren was a sensitive soul and truly wouldn't hurt a fly. So when she took the brunt of Dale's mood swings it often resulted with her in tears. Then what would happen after I'd given her a hug and told her it would all be ok; would resemble something along the lines of me hunting down Dale, telling him off, him telling me off, a cigarette and a laugh. We had, I hesitate to say for fear of being presumptuous, a relationship that resembled family rather than work colleagues. There were no silly rules and regulations as there are in offices, no disciplinary procedures. If there was a problem you had a big row then you sorted things out and you moved on. It was real life day in day out, and I loved the simplicity of it.

This particular morning as Lauren had got stuck in traffic I started work in her block and Dale started in mine. That meant I was dealing with the big guys this morning. I love all dogs no matter what shape or size; big dogs do however make me feel a little disadvantaged being as I was often half their weight. Which is of course laughable in cases such as the Chad the Akita incident; less so however if I ever found myself in a sticky situation which consisted of me versus dog.

As I'd been off work I had no idea who was in Beech block, and as I closed the gate behind me and slid the metal bar across; I was greeted with the biggest, loudest bark I'd ever heard . It vibrated through the concrete alleyway and through my legs. As I turned around I saw him; Kujo. I had heard about kujo from Lauren in the week but didn't know he'd still be in. Kujo was a St Bernard and he was absolutely beautiful. Apparently however he was choosey who he liked and who he didn't. Kujo went quiet as we stood facing each other, either side of the metal gate – a sturdy gate I was hugely grateful for. His big eyes looked into mine as his large jaw opened slowly and suddenly he let rip into a barking frenzy. Apparently this wasn't my lucky day.

"Hi Kujo boy, don't be scared I would never hurt you boy." I decided I'd start at the other end of the block and hopefully Lauren would be here in a few minutes.

At the other end I was greeted by Rocco. Rocco was a Staffordshire bull terrier. He was tan and white and such a gorgeous boy. He wasn't aggressive to people at all, a big softie; dogs on the other hand were his sworn enemy and as soon as you opened his kennel door his laps up and down the kennel ally would begin. I took a deep breath and opened his gate, about ten minutes later I'd managed to herd him into the exercise area and clean out his kennel.

"Hi babe I'm here", I heard the sweet sound of Lauren's voice from Rocco's kennel; I popped out my head.

"Hi huny, Kujo is still here then? I left your boy for you to do as he almost certainly hates me", I said with a smile.

"Aww kujo you don't hate Emma do you baby boy" Lauren scratched his chin through the kennel bars and he lapped it up, as soon as I walked over however his big bark was back.

"My god he really doesn't like you does he?" She laughed in jest. "We will have to get you both better acquainted later" she winked at me.

After cleaning out and feeding time was over we sat in the sunshine drinking tea and eating chocolate biscuits which were melting in the heat.

"Kujo really isn't that scary you know, he just takes a while to trust you then he is the biggest softie. How about we finish these then go sit in the exercise area with him?" Lauren said.

The thought made my heart race. But I decided it was a good idea, I needed to gain his trust and I had to lose my fear for that.

"Ok let's do it come on." I jumped up and headed down the kennels followed closely by Lauren; I checked a few times.

Kujo was lying down in the exercise area, panting in the sunshine, his big pink tongue hung out the side if his very large mouth. There was plenty of shade but he was clearly a sun worshipper. As we entered the gate he leaped up and came bounding over. This is it I thought, this is the end. But Kujo leapt up at Lauren and started licking her face. Lauren giggled and turned to me. "See, I told you, a big softie." I walked towards them and plucked up enough courage to hold out my hand for him to sniff me. He gave me a look as if he was weighing up his options; he then proceeded to smother my hand in licks and slobber. I laughed in relief. Thank god.

Chapter 15

Something's wrong.

I'd been feeling tired for a long time. I put it down to working harder than I'd ever worked; which also explained the weight loss. One day however, something appeared that I could not explain.

"Em!" Dave screeched at me as I dropped my cigarette and it rolled towards the brake pedal.

"Sorry I don't know what happened, can you get it for me? There's still half left on that," I said with a cheeky smile. My trusty cheeky smile often got me out of tricky situations. Dave hated me smoking in the car; Dave hated me smoking full stop but the car was a particularly touchy subject at the best of times, let alone when I'm dropping lit cigarettes inside it.

"That's weird actually that's happened a few times, don't know what's going on with my hand."

"You're a clumsy smoker that's what's going on here," Dave was not amused yet I detected a hint of retreat and a whisper of a smile.

Over the next few days my hand started to go numb, I was unusually blasé about the whole thing. I was so wrapped up in work and my relationship with Dave - which was taking a bit of a nosedive – that I just shrugged it off as a strain or something.

My relationship with Dave had always been a fiery one. We're both headstrong and stubborn which doesn't bode well for a conflict of opinion. Our arguments were always big ones; we'd make up - be ok for a few days - then have another one. This had been going on for a few weeks and it was wearing us both down. Despite the arguing and a few faltering heated words, I can safely say I think we both knew we were meant to be after all we had been through together and the trouble we had taken to be together a second time. And now here we were engaged, our future mapped out, but going through one of those rough patches people talk about. So we just kept on with the routine of work and home and hoped we could push our way through to the other side before we completely killed what we had.

I excused away my tiredness, my weight loss, but one day at work the numbing hand became impossible to ignore any longer.

"Let me just update your phone number Mrs Thompson." Bailey sat eagerly waiting as I checked him in for his stay. Bailey was a Yellow Labrador and so obedient. Once he got through our kennel doors however he was a fit of excitement and joy. The dogs loved coming here so much.

I grabbed a pen and started to take down the number...the pen kept slipping from my grasp. I laughed it off. "Sorry Mrs Thompson I will get your number down in a minute, having a few problems with this."

"What you doing girl?" Dale had unknowingly crept up behind me and had seen my futile efforts to grip the pen. "Give it here granny hand," He grinned and took the pen kindly saving me from any further embarrassment in front of the customer; subsequent to the 'granny hand' comment which of course he hadn't been able to resist.

I decided enough was enough and booked in at the emergency doctors on my day off.

"Well nothing to worry about Miss Warrington. Probably just an injury you haven't noticed or a trapped nerve." The doctor who looked young enough to be my son- bearing in mind I was 25 – put my mind right at ease.

So I plodded on, but I was growing ever weaker. My weight had dropped to under seven stone and I felt so faint most of the time. Had I been in any other job I'm sure without a doubt I'd have been off sick, but my job wasn't work, it was home. I didn't care that I got home after ten hours out of the house and had only enough energy to collapse on the sofa. I didn't care that my jeans were hanging off me, I didn't care that the fact I had no energy meant I couldn't be the efficient housewife Dave wanted; I didn't care. I loved my job more than I can say and nothing else mattered.

Lauren and I were giving one of the kennels a post stay clean. I pushed my sponge deep into the bucket of soapy bubbles and squeezed out the water. After squeezing with all my might the sponge was still heavy with water as my right hand still wasn't working. Despite my left hand becoming increasingly less redundant, it still wasn't quite up to par yet. I vigorously attacked the wall of the kennel with my sponge. I started to feel hot; very hot. It waved over me, each surge stronger than the last. My mouth began to water and the world began to spin.

"Em you ok?" I heard Lauren's voice as though she was miles away, or was I the one miles away?

"Yep, just feel a bit weird, going to go get a drink of water be back in a minute." I didn't want to say how weird I felt, I guess I was embarrassed. I tentatively stepped out of the kennel, I concentrated with all I had; one step, two step, three step...until I was in the kitchen.

The water was cold as it slid down my warm throat. I crouched against the cupboard and held my head in my hands. I don't know how long I was there; I just remember thinking I had to get back to help Lauren. So I steadied myself to my legs and made my way through the first gate into my block. Lauren was in the next block, through another two gates.

"I can't make it" I remember thinking, and opened the gate to one of the kennels; Daisy's. Daisy was a tiny black fluffy sweetheart whom I'd been having lots of cuddles with of late as it was her first stay in kennels; I'd been spoiling her just a little. I closed the gate behind me and slumped against the wall. Daisy came running over and jumped up to lick my nose. When I didn't respond as usual she sat looking puzzled and let out a small whimper. I sat on the ground so she could sit on my lap which she swiftly did. I don't know how long passed after that but at some point Lauren walked past the kennel.

"There you are what are you doing in there? My god you don't look so good." Laurens faced changed from a questioning smile to hesitant concern.

"Shall I go and get Dale?"

68

"No no I'll be ok in a minute. I'll just sit here a while n I'll be fine." I smiled weakly at my friend.

"You sure?" She asked. I nodded softly in reply. "OK well just shout if you need me ok?" I nodded once more as she walked away.

It can't have been more than ten minutes when Lauren returned.

"Come on hun, Dale wants to see you he's in reception and just wants to check you're ok."

I didn't even argue as she opened the kennel gate and helped me up. I staggered through to reception feeling as though my legs were made of lead.

"You look bloody awful what's up with you?" Dale was his usual blatant self.

"I don't know I just feel really...I don't know. I'm just so hot." I took off my second layer and held my jumper in front of me.

"Come on let's get you over to the house, come on no arguing." Dale led me over to the bungalow and opened the door. "Here lie down there a minute," he gestured towards the sofa. I remember thinking how strange it was to see Dale worried. "Denise! Denise!" Dale shouted for his wife notably concerned. She appeared from the kitchen. "She's not well she needs to see a doctor. You keep an eye on her while I call them."

I rested my head on the pillow and curled into a ball. I closed my eyes softly.

- - - - -

When I woke up Dale was smoking at the table.

"Can I have one of those?" I slowly sat up. Dale turned round and said "God you're alive then. How you feeling? Here," he handed me a cigarette and a lighter.

"I feel weird but better than before." I took a tentative drag on the cig.

"Well I've booked you in at your doctors we got to go in 20 minutes. You can leave your dogs here for a few days; get some rest."

"Thank you, I'm so sorry about this. Thanks for the offer but I really don't think I can leave my dogs, I want them with me." Over

69

the years I have had so many offers of help. The constant barking and whirlwind that was owning three dogs got a little over bearing at times. I could never bring myself to take any of them up on the break though. My house just isn't my home without my dogs.

Dale and I walked into the doctors consulting room and took a seat. The doctor was a young man whom I suspect hadn't been graduated long. I came to this conclusion after he stared blankly at me once I'd explained my symptoms, and then proceeded to search through reference books.

"Well I think you probably have a virus." That V word again. The word that appears when the doctors can't explain why you feel like you are slowly dying.

"What about my hand? That can't be a virus surely?" My voice carried a twang of impatient contempt.

"Well I don't know I think so. Just go home and rest for a week and see how you feel."

Well that was that then. To say I was fuming inside wouldn't explain the frustration that was inside me. All I wanted was some pills to fix me and to be fit to go back to work in a few days.

Yet apparently this wasn't to be the case. Home rest it was for me. Which I put up with for a few days before Dave took me to A and E.

Chapter 16

Nobody knows.

I was lying on the hospital bed waiting to see a doctor. Dave was sat on a chair next to me. I could barely keep my eyes open. I felt as though every inch of energy had been vacuumed from my body. Dave was a fun hospital friend; cracking jokes and making me smile to take my mind from where I lay. I'd never been in hospital; never broken a bone, never had an operation. So being in this clinical environment with that oh so familiar smell that triggers the sense of unease, was quite daunting. What is it about hospitals that despite your nostrils wringing with the smell of disinfectant you always feel dirty? The sheets on the bed stiff and discoloured, the blue blanket that is thinning and is a few years off reaching antique status. It all surrounds you as you lay there too ill to move and go home to your big warm duvet on your comfy clean bed.

"Hello Emma I'm Doctor Smith how can we help you today?" Another doctor. I explained my symptoms once again, it was getting tedious. Little did I know that through the night I'd have to tell three more doctors the ins and outs of my mystery illness as I got passed from one specialist to the next as none of them could determine what was wrong with me. I began to question what exactly qualified one to be a doctor – perhaps reading a first aid manual sufficed these days.

During my 24 hour stay I was prodded and poked, had bloods taken, performed strange tasks such as touching my nose and was discharged with a view to me coming back for an MRI scan. MRI – isn't that what they use to diagnose brain tumours? I cried and cried; convinced that this is what I had. It would explain the lack of functionality in my hand, the drained feeling, and the fact no-one could see what was wrong with me.

It was a long two weeks sat at home waiting for the scan, but the day had finally arrived. I'd never had an MRI before and the pure sight of it made my tummy flutter. It was a long tunnel with a sliding bed inside it. As I lay on flat on my back the nurse placed what I can only describe as a cage over my face. She had gone through all the ins and outs of the scan with me before I lay down. She was patient and had a kind voice. As I slid inside the tunnel holding my panic button I could hear my heartbeat pounding. I closed my eyes so as not to see how trapped I was; claustrophobia was creeping in. I don't know how long I was in there, but after what seemed like an age I heard the nurse say through my headphones; "Ok Emma we're bringing you out now". I was glad it was all over, now it was time to wait to hear my fate.

I decided to go back to work; I was feeling a little better and was going stir crazy sitting around waiting for a phone call. The use of my hand was returning very gradually and the rest seemed to have eased my tiredness.

Being back with my second family made everything seemed a little brighter. Denise had told me to take it steady and ask if I needed help. Dale was surprisingly easy going and agreeable towards me and Lauren was her usual lovely self. I'd seen another side to Dale through this. He may have appeared aloof but deep down he cared about us all more than he liked to admit – and we all felt the same way about him.

The day things began to unfold began like any other, but ended with me staring at a webpage in tears.

"Emma!" Dale shouted me from the kitchen door. I made my way up the kennels past all the adorable faces jumping up to greet me as I walked through. "I'll be back in a bit guys."

"Yep what it is?" I closed the last gate and walked into the kitchen where Dale was already walking out.

"Come on my new bird cage has arrived come and help me put it up." I sighed; Dale and his birds. He had an African gray parrot which he had just bought for god knows how much money and apparently I was switching from kennel maid to cage assembler for an hour or so. I didn't mind one bit though. How can I explain this? Dale was like a secondary father figure to me in a way, only neither he nor I shared any obligation to one another than that of employer and employee. I already had a wonderful father and he had his gorgeous daughter Zoe so we didn't need each other in that way. But to call him simply my boss didn't seem apt. Dale's praise was always something that was hard to gain, therefore something I constantly aimed for. So being considered worthy of helping him build something was a good feeling.

We eventually got the blasted thing together and Annie the Parrot seemed very happy with our handy work.

"I'm so fed up of waiting for these damn results. What if something's wrong with me?" Dale and I were enjoying a well earned cup of tea and a cigarette at his dining table.

"There's nowt up with you girl, if there was they would have rang you by now so don't be fretting. Ring them if you want." Dale got up and handed me the phone.

I dialled the hospital number while Dale went to feed the dogs.

"Oh hello Miss Warrington" a man who sounded in his fifties or sixties answered my redirected call. "Yes we did find something on the MRI but I'm not at liberty to discuss it with you over the phone. There will be an appointment in the post for you to see a consultant."

The words took my breath away for a moment.

"Miss Warrington? Are you still there?"

"You can't just say that and leave me for weeks waiting for an appointment. What sort of thing did you find? Is it something that can be treated?" Or am I going to die? That's what I wanted to ask.

"There are treatments for what you have yes but I really can't tell you anymore. I'm sorry your appointment won't be long and then you can discuss all this with your consultant."

"Right, ok. Thank you. Bye."

I hung up the phone and my hands found their way up to my mouth. Oh my god, I had something; something that shows up on a brain scan. The tears slowly, quietly fell from my eyes, down my hands and landed in small pools on the table.

Dale walked back in and saw this. He reached into his pocket and handed me a cigarette from his pack.

"Come on then, tell me what they said."

– – – – –

73

As soon as I got in I turned on the laptop. Google can be a wonderful tool and today it was going to serve me well. I typed in my symptoms and trailed through streams of information: Brain tumour symptoms, Parkinson's disease, then came ME and MS. As I read through the symptoms of both illnesses I remember turning to Dave and saying;

"This is it; this is what I've got. I think I've got this MS thing."

Chapter 17

Diagnosis – the relief, the fear, the sentence.

After ten days – consequential of booking in with the consultant privately at a cost to my parents – they and I were on our way to the appointment. Dave was at work but I had orders to ring him as soon as I knew anything.

My dad pulled up outside the hospital. He had driven us there but decided to stay in the car. I think all this was killing him; watching his little girl suffer, knowing something was very wrong but unable to do anything about it. Mum and I walked up the big concrete steps up to the sliding doors. I could hear sirens in the distance. I was having a second attack of illness by this point. I could barely walk from the feeling of exhaustion. Mum held my arm and helped me over to reception. The receptionist was around fifty and had short white hair like a powder puff.

"Yes can I help you?" You could tell this was a private hospital by the way they made us feel like outsiders. We obviously didn't have that private healthcare 'look'.

We booked in and got called through more or less immediately; now you could definitely tell we weren't in an NHS hospital. As we followed the man who had called us down a long corridor, I'd already decided I didn't like him. Perhaps it was the fact he was walking so fast he had to keep stopping and waiting for me. The man could see I was struggling but made me feel like it was a terrible inconvenience for him.

We walked into the small consulting room and took a seat. Now the consultant was opposite me I examined the man set to deliver this bad news to me. He was: white, mid forties, greying hair though I suspect it was once a mousy blond. He had a stocky build but wasn't overweight. He wore a grey suit and blue tie and spoke with an accent I can't quite put my finger on but what I did recognise, quite clearly, was the tone of superiority.

"So we saw you at Lincoln Hospital two weeks ago and there you reported..." He went on to read my notes out to me; like I didn't know what had been happening, this was my life we were talking about.

"So I suggest we do some more tests and continue from there, do you have any questions?" We had been in the room no more than five minutes. I had been dreading this moment for days; but at least I would get answers – or so I thought.

"What, that's it?" The tears pricked in my eyes and I fought so hard but they trained down my cheeks one after the other; faster and faster.

"I thought you would be telling me what's wrong with me. I thought you had found something on the MRI? Do you not think its MS?" I was angry and all the frustration and tears came at once.

The consultant seemed taken aback from my last question.

"Well, MS is one of the strong possibilities yes but that's why I need to do more tests to be sure and do some more blood tests as well to make sure it is not something else. So I will arrange those and send you the appointments in the post. I would be grateful if you could come to Sheffield as it is where I'm based and is a much better hospital with better equipment. Is that something you would be willing to do?" The doctor looked at my mother rather than me. Clearly I was incapable of making decisions now there was something wrong inside my brain...and so it began.

\- - - - -

I lay on the sofa with my eyes closed. The words from my Google searches of the last few weeks whirled through my mind.

'MS is a condition where the immune system attacks its own body, primarily the nerves. Our nerves have a protective sheath around them and the damage done depends on how far through this the immune cells get during their attack.'

The attack I was suffering from now was on my eyes. I couldn't focus on anything or change focus as the pain behind my eyes was excruciating. So there I was; unable to watch TV, read a book, use the laptop, I basically had to lay there and wish the day away, oh and worry about whether my eyesight would ever be the same. This was a difficult time and I don't know how I'd have made it through without my dogs. Ronnie, Tess and Megan would come and snuggle up next to me on the sofa; I didn't need my eyes to see the beauty in them. I'd feel their warm bodies against mine and bury my face in their soft fur and know that I wasn't alone, that they didn't judge me or pity me; they were just there, just as they'd always been.

My mum came to our house a lot now to take care of me while Dave was at work. This was a 40 mile return journey for her as well as the fact she was working and keeping a house herself; I felt awful. The fact was though I needed her and I wouldn't have been coping without her or Dave.

It was a Monday morning and as I'd opened my eyes the room had began to spin around me.

"Babe I've got to go now do you want anything before I do?" Dave popped his head around our bedroom door; dressed in his red work uniform.

"Please don't leave me," my meek voice begged as tears began to fall down my face.

"Oh Em, why? Are you still dizzy?" He walked over to me. "I have to go you know that, we need the money."

"But I don't know how I'm going to even get up." I hated asking him but I really didn't want to do this alone.

I knew Dave was stuck between a rock and a hard place; if he stayed at home he didn't get paid the money we desperately needed now we had lost my wage, if he went to work I could fall down the stairs and hurt myself or worse. He left the room for a while. When he came back he began taking off his uniform.

"Are you staying?" I asked.

"Course I am I can't leave you like this can I? But we'll have to make some plans for tomorrow because if I don't go in then we won't be eating next week." He smiled at me trying to make light of it but I knew it was true; we were really in trouble.

I have always been a proud person, I take after my mother and father on that one, so this whole thing was killing me, I hated every second. I just wanted it to end; I just wanted to be me again.

77

My appointment for Sheffield had arrived. The attack on my eyes had thankfully retreated leaving a twinge of pain behind my eyes when I refocused, but this wasn't a patch on what I had been used to. This day just so happened to be the day we had the heaviest snowfall that we have had in years; and we had a 150 mile return journey ahead of us. Thankfully Dave had booked the day off and drove us there; through hours of traffic jams, icy roads and snowstorms. I remember distinctly the Westlife song 'Safe' coming on the radio. There's a line in the song which says 'I will keep you safe' – Dave sang this to me laughing as we skidded and crawled along the roads. It has since become a little anthem of ours. Dave has the ability to make even the most frightening or tedious times that little bit more fun. Mum came with us too which I was so glad about. There's nothing like a mum's presence – even at the age of 25 – to comfort you.

We eventually arrived and the hospital was enormous. But we found our department and began the long day of blood tests, brain scans, and tests I cannot even recall the name of.

The last test I had was the one I'd been dreading since I got my list of appointments for the day; the lumbar puncture. I had googled all about it – naturally – and filled myself with horror stories and fear – naturally. I hated needles; just going for a blood test was a heart thumping, psych myself up for a week, kind of occasion. So as I lay on the bed; my knees tucked up to my chin and waited for the nurse to put a needle in my spinal column; I felt overcome with fear. My mum held my hand and she injected the local anaesthetic into my skin. "Ahhh!" I let out a painful howl as the needle hit a nerve. This was something that didn't usually happen apparently – well lucky me. The look on my mum's face was more painful than the needle was. Since all this started I had seen the worry and pain become part of her. I can't imagine what it must be like to watch your child go through this, but the look on her face said it was agony. The pity I saw hurt even more. I didn't want this – I didn't want any of this; I just wanted to go back to my life.

We arrived home at 12:30 am after sitting in standstill jams and skidding more than driving, we had left that morning at 6:30 am. It had been the longest most painful day of my life and the pain in my back lasted the duration of the night and in the morning all our faces carried the look of relief that that day was behind us.

After a couple of weeks mum and I were sitting in my doctor's consultation room once again. He had called me in to discuss the results of the tests. This time I walked out with the diagnosis of Multiple Sclerosis. To finally have a label to put on how I was feeling was a relief; relief that I wasn't imagining all of these symptoms, that they would have to believe me and not send me away with a common virus. At the same time I wished I did have a virus; that what I had would go in a week or two. But I knew – I'd known for weeks - I had MS. It had just been getting the so called professionals to believe me and not think I was some sort of hypochondriac. Yet now it was here; now it was final and permanent, it was like the busyness, the worry, the appointments, the tests; it all just stopped; my whole world just stopped. What I was left with was a sentence; a sentence of uncertainty and predictions for what my future would hold. They didn't know if my disease would progress quickly or slowly or when or if I'd lose the ability to walk. But what they did know was that it would at some point progress, and that at some point, I may or may not be in a wheelchair, lose my bladder control or the ability to open a bag of crisps. So in one breath all the uncertainty regarding what was wrong with me was gratefully taken away; but in the next breath a new uncertainty rooted firmly in my thoughts and made my fears its home.

The days and weeks that followed were extremely difficult. Difficult; that doesn't really cover the rollercoaster of emotions and frustrations I experienced but for that there are just no words that would do justice to the waves that rolled through me from day to day. I tried to think positively; I wasn't dying, I didn't have cancer and I had family and friends who cared deeply for me. But on the bad days – the days my friends were going out to dance the night away and I couldn't go, the days mum took me shopping to lift my spirits and we had to return home after an hour because I was exhausted – those days were dark ones. I would sit and cry in secret as I didn't want to cause my family any more hurt. Yet I was not alone. On these days Megan would come and sit quietly next to me. I remember one day in particular I'd grown tired of being useless. Dave would come home from a day's work and have all the house work to do as I lay on the sofa too ill to move. So that day I thought mind over matter how hard can it be? I pottered around doing small jobs until the fatigue was so strong I could hardly breathe. I collapsed in a ball of tears and frustration on the floor in front of the sofa. Megan hopped onto the sofa and gently rested her soft brown head on my shoulder. Her warm nose nuzzled into my neck. Megan was not a 'licky dog' she was polite and would just gently sniff you. But today she, ever so softly, licked the tears from my face until a smile crept on to my face. This moment showed me something magical lies in the connection between dogs and humans and will always be one of the best feelings of my life.

Chapter 18

Letting go and learning to fight.

I missed work. I loved my job and was desperate to go back. It's funny; all my life I had wished I didn't have to work. But they were my old jobs, before I had found the job of my dreams. Dale and Denise had been wonderful through all of this. They weren't cross that I couldn't come in, despite having to work twice as hard to do my share. I rang them frequently to keep them updated but mostly because I missed them. They felt like my second family rather than my bosses and I missed everything about working for them.

My mum had been gently telling me for weeks that I wouldn't be able to go back to work; the job was just too manual and my body couldn't take it anymore. I, of course, insisted I would go back, I would; I had to. But I had been off work for months now and I felt as though I owed it to Dale and Denise to let them hire someone else. That phone call to tell them was the hardest I'd ever had to make and when I hung up the phone the tears were uncontrollable. That job was my life and I loved everything about it. I'd felt at home working at Pond View; that I'd finally found where I belonged and it had been torn from me. I began to fall back into my black hole of nothing until one night, after smoking a cigarette under the stars, I came back into my living room and sat next to Dave.

"Let's get married." I looked at Dave who was staring at the TV; he smirked.

"We are already engaged baby, what are you talking about?"

"No I mean lets actually get married, in a few weeks. I have the money from Grandma's inheritance; what do you think?"

Now I had his attention. Dave turned and looked at me with a smile of puzzlement. "What's the rush? I mean I want to obviously, but why a few weeks?"

I hung my head. I'd hoped I wouldn't have to say all this.

"Dave we don't know how long my legs are going to work for, I could have an attack tomorrow and I could never walk again. I have to walk down the aisle, I can't go down it in a wheelchair I just can't. But Dave I want you to know that if this isn't the life you want anymore, if I'm not the girl you want anymore, it's ok; I'll understand. You proposed before I had MS and the last thing I want is for you to marry me out of pity."

"What are you like? I love you Emma, just because you have MS now doesn't change the fact you're the girl I fell in love with. Even if you are a grumpy madam lately," he said with a cheeky grin.

I smiled back at him and playfully pushed him.

"Well let's get the laptop out then, we have a lot of planning to do."

– – – – –

I woke up the next day feeling positive for the first time in months; I had a purpose – I had a wedding to plan.

My days were going to be filled with giving people good news after weeks of bad news, searching for venues, dresses, cakes; it was going to be girl heaven and I couldn't wait.

Not being able to wait is a certain trait of mine; so when I made the phone call to my mum she was shocked but knew her attempts to persuade me to wait a few months were futile. So it began.

– – – – –

Dave and I were on route to view a venue a few miles out of the city. As we arrived and drove up the enormous concrete drive surrounded on all sides by green grass and tall blooming trees, we both looked at each other and thought 'oh yes'.

We met the owner in reception and the place was just as spectacular inside as out. The ceilings were so high and period features were everywhere you looked. She showed us the room where we'd be married and it was a little disappointing; just a small square room with a fireplace. However I excused this as the room where we would eat was lovely; big feature window, gorgeous fireplace; I could definitely see us all laughing, eating and making speeches in there. Then we made our way up a grand staircase to view the bridal suite and it certainly had the wow factor; a stunning four poster bed, big feature window with views over the grounds and one hell of a bathroom.

Dave and I were smitten with the place; yet there was a nagging thought in both our minds; we can't afford this. So as we broached the matter with the owner the sum of £5500 stung in our throats as we tried to respond. If we really stretched we could afford it but there was the matter of principle. Despite handing over all that money the owner wouldn't give us occupancy of the hotel bar for the night as they wouldn't turn regulars away, or whoever else turned up on the evening either for that matter. We also had to book all twelve bedrooms to secure the booking. Now the place was nice but it wasn't a castle and only a castle would do if I was going to be casting principle aside. So that was that, it wasn't our venue.

Back home, on the laptop, Dave had an idea. "Search for The White Hart Hotel, I did my work experience there and it was nice, like really nice."

- - - - -

As we walked hand in hand towards the hotel, the bells chimed from the cathedral around the corner. The deep heavy ringing travelled through me. My eyes followed the sound and I saw the symbolic towers standing tall behind the surrounding shops and bars.

The hotel exterior was white with black frames. I looked above me where balconies protruded large windows. We made our way through the grand revolving doors and I immediately felt as though I were in a London boutique hotel. In front of us was an upmarket bar with black tub chairs and mahogany tables. The barman was dressed in a crisp while shirt and black waistcoat. Reception was marked to the left where we waited on lavishly upholstered chairs for our representative to arrive.

"Well this is posh," I whispered to Dave.

"Yeah, it's had a re – vamp since I was here too."

A blonde woman approached us.

"Hi there you must be Dave and Emma, I'm Hannah I'm the wedding co-ordinator here at the White Hart; shall we have a seat in the bar?"

As we followed her back through to the bar, I noticed her black patent shoes clanging on the wooden floor as she struggled to keep them on her feet. They say you make a judgement on someone within seconds of meeting them and well; I didn't like her. Perhaps she was having a busy day but I felt as though we were just too much effort for her. She went over the package we were interested in which was a winter offer. She only had one date left; Saturday February 12th. Despite that being only six weeks away we were definitely interested.

Hannah showed us the room in which we'd be married and I have to say I was a little underwhelmed. On the left hand side of the room was a bar, which on the one hand would mean only our guests would be around us as we celebrated our day; no strangers invading the wedding party. On the other hand though did I really want a bar adjacent to me as I walked down the aisle? No I did not. The room was dressed for a wedding, which Hannah informed us was happening the next day. The white covered chairs with pink bows were laid out to create an aisle down the middle. At the head of the aisle was a white covered table with candle stands either side.

Still feeling disappointed I followed Hannah through the double doors at the back of the room; where I immediately felt better. This was the room where we would eat and do speeches and it was beautiful. The tables were all dressed in white linen with blooming flower centre pieces. The top table sat beneath an extravagant gold mirror below which was a white feature fireplace. In the centre of the room a brass candelabra hung from the ceiling. It was stunning.

We agreed to talk it over at home and give Hannah a ring later.

"So what did you really think?" I asked Dave as we walked through the revolving doors.

"I thought it was gorgeous didn't you?" His face was the picture of excitement. I told him my disappointment with the ceremony room but I was swaying towards making the booking as the reception suite was everything I dreamed of. We were having another look outside when it hit me; a wave of love for my man. As I looked at him I realised I'd marry him anywhere and he loved this place and as long as I got to look like a princess and say my vows to him I was happy.

"Let's go back in and book it," I turned to Dave as I walked towards the doors. He followed me with a smile on his face and his hand slipped into mine.

Chapter 19

I do.

My mum; once over the shock of having only six weeks until her daughter's wedding, was a god send. She made the invitations for me, organised days for us to sort out the menu tasting, the flowers, the seating plan, the list goes on. My other little wedding star was Maggie.

I met Maggie working at a preschool in a children's centre; she was the beautiful exotic receptionist. She came to England from Spain seven years ago to study and never wanted to leave. I ask her constantly why rainy old England trumps sunny Spain but never get any sense out of her. I suppose home is where your heart is and luckily for me and everyone else who knew her; Maggie's heart was in England. Maggie was one of those people who would do anything for you; who went out of her way to make you feel special, she also made your sides split with laughter. Having English as a second language Maggie got certain things confused and coupled with her accent you spent half the time in fits of giggles. One occasion in particular springs to mind: During a very formal meeting Maggie was taking notes, after running out of paper she asked; "Does anyone have some paper I need a sheet?" Say this in a Spanish accent and all will become clear. Having said that her English was beautifully fluent and the tiny mistakes livened up the dullest of moments.

I was not great with computers so Maggie helped with all the technical jobs for the wedding and turned out to be a great planner and organiser. Between Maggie and Mum they had me all sorted and relatively stress free.

I had chosen Maggie as one of my bridesmaids, along with my best friend Kerry – who had gotten me through some of the worst days of my life, she's always there whenever I need her; I can tell her anything. It's safe to say Kerry is more like the sister I never had than a friend. I'd chosen two more; Dave's niece Yasmin and

Kerry's niece Mia – a little girl who truly deserved to be a princess for the day. All my beautiful girls needed beautiful dresses so we hit the shops. This turned out to be more stressful than choosing my dress. With so many different sizes finding dresses to suit them all proved a mission and I was still suffering with the fatigue following my attacks but in the end we did it.

A few days before, completely by chance, mum and I had found my dress. After visiting the White Hart for one of many appointments we saw a wedding shop across the road.

"Let's just have a look in here, see what kind of dresses you like," Mum said. The lady inside radiated warmth and kindness and she picked out some dresses for me to try on.

"This one would suit you perfectly, it's a little big for you but we can have it altered."

I put the dress on...a little big? You could have fit three of me in this dress. I staggered out of the changing room and stood in front of my mum and the owner. My face was clearly the picture of pessimism.

"Here, let me show you what it could look like", the woman stood behind me, gathered in all the excess dress so it was tight then said, "There, have a look in the mirror."

What I saw looking back at me was a princess. The ivory dress had a halter neck strap which was lined with small satin flowers. The sweetheart neckline skimmed the top of my breasts; there was a lot room in there as a size 18 lady would clearly have a fuller bosom than my modest 32B cup. From there the dress clung to my tiny waist and at my hips flowed out gradually in an A line covered gently with soft ivory netting. On my hip bone was the most beautiful ivory satin flower.

I looked at mum to see what she thought and her eyes were full of tears, her hand resting over her mouth.

"You like it then? I asked with a smile.

"Emma you look absolutely beau..." Her voice choked and the tears found their way down her cheeks.

We looked at other dresses but it was clear the first one was the one.

How anyone can make a size 18 dress into an 8 I will never know but the fitter did and it was perfect. The chest area was still a little generous but hopefully people wouldn't be giving that too much attention.

The wedding was about two weeks away when I started having another attack. My left leg was starting to go numb from the foot up. At the moment I could still walk fine but as the nature of MS goes; you never know what might have changed when you wake up in the morning. It would be sod's ironic law that I'd rushed to get married so I could walk down the aisle only to have an attack which left my left leg unable to function and I'd have to do down in a wheelchair. I wouldn't do it; I'd cancel the whole day and lose all the money for our wedding, but I know my pride wouldn't let me sit there with everyone pitying me.

My consultant put me on steroids to reduce the inflammation in my brain. One of the side effects of steroids is the fact you cannot stop eating. I'd even be getting up in the middle of the night for a biscuit, it was ridiculous. This of course meant that on top of worrying about my leg I was also extremely concerned that I wouldn't fit in to my now incredibly tiny dress. After having another fitting the dress zipped up but my lungs screamed for oxygen after ten minutes of having it on. Alas, there was nothing that could be done now I would just have to hope it would all work out.

Hope; alone the feeling can be a wonderful thing. Though hope is so often closely followed by disappointment it was hard to find any comfort.

It was the day before the wedding and Maggie, Mum and I, after our last appointment at the venue, were having some lunch in a local restaurant. The incessant fatigue I was suffering was becoming impossible to ignore. Even having a conversation drained every ounce of energy from me. This was leaving me a little snappy; in all honesty I was a complete petulant nightmare. My mum took me home where Dave was waiting with an overnight bag for me; I was booked in at the White Hart for a girly pre wedding night with Maggie.

"I'm not going." I walked past him and up to my bed.

"Where's Megan?" I called on the way up. I could hear Mum and Dave talking about me.

"I just don't know how she's going to do it." Mum spoke with a drained voice laced with dejection.

"What do u mean? She'll be fine don't panic. You go up I just need to let Megs out the kitchen as the lady of the house has called for her," I could tell from his voice he was smiling.

Dave has always been the type of guy never to take life too seriously; this being a more than necessary trait when marrying a high maintenance worrier like myself.

I heard Megan's familiar gallop coming up the stairs. She jumped on the bed and snuggled into me wagging her tail. Now I felt better. I smiled at her big brown eyes looking into mine. Whenever she was next to me all my frustration and despair vanished in an instant.

"What's this I hear about you being a mardy moo then?" Dave appeared in the doorway with a cheeky grin.

"You can't stay here with me can you its tradition, I thought that was important to you?"

"But I just want to stay here and have cuddles with you and Megan." My bottom lip was officially making its appearance. "I'm not going to see Megs for two whole nights and I don't think I can do it, not now, I feel so..."

"...mooey?" Dave's cheeky smile was back. "Come on I'll be there waiting for you tomorrow and we will have our amazing day together then we can go collect Megs, Ronnie and Tess first thing from the kennels.

I'd booked them all into Pond View; I wouldn't trust any other kennels with my babies.

I got up and made my way into Dave's arms. As he locked his big biceps around me everything faded away. When he was near me I felt safe, loved, protected.

After more doggie cuddles and a last one from my hubby to be, Mum and I made our way to the hotel. Maggie was meeting me there for a few hours but I'd decided to spend overnight by myself, get some much needed rest. At least that had been the plan, like any other bride I imagine, I spent most of the night tossing and turning.

As the sun glistened through the bedroom curtain I opened my eyes, this was it; my wedding day had arrived.

- - - - -

I was up at 7:30 so by the time my hair and makeup were done and my hotel suite was filled with bridesmaids and busyness I was shattered. The fatigue was beginning to make it hard to breathe let alone anything else but I kept trying; making conversation with my mum, my girls. Before I knew it the shopkeeper arrived with my dress and she and my mum were helping me into it.

As they zipped up the back the fatigue went from bad to worse; much worse. Heat waved over me and that familiar feeling rose in my throat and my mouth began watering.

"I think, I'm going to be sick", my weak voice was only just heard. The wedding dress lady just had time to whip the top of my dress down before I ran to the bathroom.

"Are you ok?" Mum appeared behind me as I hugged the toilet crying. I made my way out to the hotel bedroom and sat against the wall feeling as though I really shouldn't be anywhere but a hospital bed. My mum disappeared for a while. I guessed she'd gone downstairs to tell people that I may not be coming down.

I was sitting there and something just clicked. I knew there was no option but to; get up, get my make up sorted and get this ridiculously tight dress zipped up and make my way downstairs. So when mum came back she couldn't believe I was ready to go. She positioned my veil and before I knew it I was in the consulting room with the registrar. As dad took my arm he told me I looked beautiful; he looked so proud, I think he was trying very hard to hide any worry or pity and that was just what I needed. I watched my beautiful bridesmaids walk down the aisle then I took a deep breath. I turned the corner and my eyes searched for Dave...there he was. The tension, the anticipation, the fear; it all faded the instant my eyes found his. A silly smile crept onto my face and the rest as they say is history. Saying my vows I couldn't have meant them more. I couldn't get though a single day without Dave by my side; however many times our fiery natures cause stern words, the fact remains my world is a better place with him in it.

The adrenaline didn't last nearly long enough as when it faded the unbearable fatigue and nausea where back with vengeance. I made the heart breaking decision to retire to my room for the meal. Dave came up to wake me for the speeches and they were beautiful. After a rest I felt so much better, by the time the evening party came and I'd gotten myself out of the dress, I was even drinking and dancing. My dad came over to me.

"You feel better now don't you?"

"I really do, it's like some sort of miracle." I really was in disbelief.

"Well, you know that Michelle woman I work with; she said she would send you some Reiki around 4 o'clock." As I mulled over his words I realised this was around the time I'd retired to my room over the meal. I'd known nothing about this. Dad had told me about Michelle before though; she was a psychic and a Reiki healer. As I understood it Reiki draws on energy around us and those trained in Reiki can channel this energy into you; even at a great distance.

I was a strong believer in the powers of psychics and that our soul remains after we pass and that some stay around us whilst others go into the next world. I hadn't heard much about Reiki but after the unexplainable improvement of my crippling fatigue, I certainly wanted to know more now.

Chapter 20

Taking control.

I remember lying there with my eyes closed. The warmth of the sun on my skin had relaxed every muscle in my body. I heard the sea lapping in the distance and the splashes of people swimming in the pool beside me. I thought 'this is the life'. I looked over at my husband and a warm feeling filled my heart; no matter how bad things were I knew I had him by my side. We had jetted off to Tenerife for our honeymoon and a week of sun was blissful; it was especially helping my MS.

Sunlight, I'd learnt from my friend Google, is our main source of vitamin D and it plays an important role in MS. Research had shown that countries further from the equator had higher levels of people suffering from MS. This had been linked to vitamin D levels as well as levels of saturated fats.

I was certainly eating well and spending all day bathing in sunlight and it was clearly agreeing with me.

I was starting to learn a lot about my illness because the more I knew the better chance I had of beating this thing. I'd left the UK with an MS relapse and when I came back after a week of sun in Tenerife; I was no longer feeling the numbness in my leg and even my fatigue had improved. If the vitamin D thing was true what else was there that I didn't know? So I read...and read...and read.

I was finding that, as with many other illnesses, there were things that helped and things that made it much worse. One thing I found, which I felt shocked and appalled that no doctor told me about, was that diet plays a big part in the severity of MS.

I learnt that the immune system has two responses; one is what kick starts the immune system to attack and defend; Th1, the other dampens it down and restores balance; Th2. MS involves the immune system attacking the nerves. It is suggested that different foods, in particular fats, can encourage the two responses. I took in the words in front of me:

"Fatty acids are the basic building blocks for the chemicals the immune system uses in these responses...Saturated (animal) fats and omega 6 (vegetable) fatty acids tip the balance towards the Th1 response. Omega 3 fatty acids (fish and flaxseed oils) tip the balance towards a Th2 response." (Jelinek, G. 2010. p66).

So for people with MS like me, this research suggests you really are what you eat. In my mind, this was an element of control I could take back. I could follow the diet plan and hopefully create my own medication.

In the midst of all this I was also deciding on a choice of treatment options available from my consultant. All of which involved injecting myself. My hatred of needles coupled with this information had me trembling to the core.

Back in the UK on my next visit to my consultant I mentioned the research I had found on diet and told him the book I'd been reading. I told him about the Professor that lead the study on saturated fat and MS beginning in 1949 but lasting many years. My consultant seemed very flippant over the matter and said he'd never heard of it. That day I started to see the medical world in a new and corrupted light. If what the researcher was proposing was correct, it meant results of the diet were equivalent and in some cases better than taking any of the medications available. This would result in a loss of the one thing that our world revolves around; money. For MS sufferers though, it would be life changing; no side effects from drugs, nothing unnatural in the body and better results for both life quality and little or no disability. I couldn't and wouldn't believe that my consultant knew less about research than I did and arrived at the conclusion that change was too difficult and costly for the NHS so they stuck with what they had; with what paid wages.

I decided to give the diet a go. I also decided, after a lot of bombarding from family and friends; that I would go on one of the treatments too.

The diet wasn't easy. I am a chocolate addict; I have a sweet tooth and this diet did not allow that. I couldn't eat so many of the things I had eaten before and I only had the will power to last a few months doing the diet as the specifications demanded. During this time however I was better than I had been in a long time. I had only one relapse and it was very mild compared to the three I had had in the last seven months. I decided I'd still kept saturated fat to a minimum where possible and my attacks have been nowhere near as severe as before the diet and my fatigue is easier to manage. The fatigue didn't magically disappear but I found that if I planned out my day including long rest breaks; I could do more of the things that made me feel normal again.

The book also recommended exercise and meditation in conjunction with the diet. I'm pretty sure walking three dogs constituted as exercise so meditation was the next mission.

A few weeks later my dad sent me for a reading with his friend Michelle; the woman who sent me Reiki on my wedding day. She told me more about Reiki as a self treatment and said she even saw me practicing Reiki on animals in the future. I felt guided, supported, inspired. I went home and Googled until I found a Reiki course in my town. I booked onto it - it started in two weeks; there'd been only one place left which I took as a sign it was meant for me. I felt as though everything was coming together to guide me on the right path.

–––––

There was a knock at the door. The postman delivering a parcel was a very loud event in our house. I still cannot believe how much noise two little terriers can make. Megan isn't a barky dog, my girl just followed them around frantically as they relayed from the window to the door and back again.

After the 'intruder' had left the property and the guys had settled down, I unwrapped my parcel; 'Animal Reiki'. I'd ordered a book from the internet to find out more about Reiki and animals. I found it hard to believe people paid to have a treatment of faith for themselves let alone for their animals. As I'm sure you are aware by now; animals are equals to me, but few shared my opinion. I read the book in two days. I was riveted by the amazing stories of the human – animal connection Reiki can bring out.

Animals haven't lost their connection with Mother Nature. They know deep in their instincts that the world is bigger than them. You only have to observe a pack of wolves to see that. The unity in the pack is strong and they will work together to protect each other from danger, they kill only what they need to survive, they prepare for winter for months and have a deep respect for the power of mother nature's weather. But most incredible of all is that they can tell when something is coming, from a knowing; a sixth sense.

When there have been hurricanes, earthquakes, the tsunami; animals in the area knew long before humans did that it was coming. Dogs would be found hiding under the table barking or trying to run away, wild animals could be seen fleeing their territories, clearly stricken with panic. After the tsunami in 2004, people reported seeing animals, about an hour before it hit, running to forests and higher ground, some reported seeing animals climbing trees. But how did they know? I'm sure scientists would explain away elements of it, but the fact remains that animals are more attuned to their environment than we are.

So after reading my book I decided to see what Tessie thought of all this Reiki business. Tess had suffered with a problem tummy since we rescued her from the RSPCA; perhaps the reason she ended up there in the first place. She would be sick frequently, at least once a day; the vet said it was something to do with overactive stomach acid. We had tried everything to no avail, so why not Reiki too.

I was in bed reading the book with Tessie asleep next to me. I gently placed my hands about an inch above her tummy. Tess opened her eyes, sniffed my hands then lay back down. I imagined a golden energy, as the book had explained, flowing from me into her, cocooning her stomach. My palms went very hot; my head started to spin, so after a few minutes I stopped and fell asleep next to my girl.

It was a few days later that I noticed Tess hadn't been sick since that night; coincidence? Perhaps; but I didn't think so.

I began my Reiki training a week later and the woman running the classes, Dee, was wonderful. She made me feel at ease instantly, as did the other five people in my class. Dee also smoked so it gave me a little extra one on one time with her when we had our cheeky breaks. My MS obviously came up and Dee said that Reiki would be so good for me and she thought the idea to Reiki animals was a beautiful one. She told me about her experience of giving Reiki to a horse and her comments were remarkable. She claimed after the treatment the horse spoke in her mind and said thank you. The owner phoned days later to tell Dee that the horse's ailment was healed. To the unspiritual mind that probably sounds far – fetched, but after my experience with Tess, who still hadn't had another sickness episode; I believed every word. Speaking of which Dee explained why I felt so drained afterwards. The energy of Reiki is usually only accessible after you have been attuned by a Reiki master. But sometimes if you have a natural gift you can access the energy needed to heal. The training provided gives you practical skills to protect your own energy from being sucked into the body you are treating and from becoming ungrounded from mother earth. This must have been what happened when I treated Tess, I gave her all of my energy as well as the Reiki; there was no wonder her stomach problem responded so well to the treatment.

I learnt that Reiki was discovered long ago by the Japanese. The man who discovered Reiki was called Dr Mikao Usui. He was a university principle in Japan as well as a Christian preacher. One day a student asked him if he could duplicate the healing Christ famously performed by lying on hands. Dr Usui replied that he could not, but resigned from his job to travel all over the world, visiting different religions, to find the answer to the mystery. His journey was an incredible one which peaked with him in deep meditation on a mountain which lasted for 21 days. On the last day on the mountain a light appeared through the clouds; it grew brighter and brighter until he contemplated running away. The light, which he felt had an intelligent presence, hit him in the centre of his forehead with such force he almost fell over. Dr Usui knew all he had worked towards had become real. On his way down the mountain he stubbed his toe; instinctively he placed his hands over his foot where upon his toe was healed.

This story is one hard to believe, I know, but one thought stuck with me. If healing through hands has never been a reality then why is it that we instinctively put our hands straight to the area we injure? Whether it's a stubbed toe like Dr Usui or a banged head - we put our hands straight to it. When we have a headache we cocoon our forehead in our palms as do we with a toothache or an earache. The more you think about it the less implausible this story becomes. Reiki, I believe, has been around for a very, very long time, back when some knew how to use a much higher percentage of their brains. It is said we only use a fraction of our brains. It would explain why some people are cleverer than others, some people are labelled geniuses; perhaps they just have the ability to access more of their brain. The same point can be made for people who have unexplainable 'gifts' such as clairvoyants, psychics, Reiki healers.

Dave supported me in training to be a Reiki practitioner but he's a sceptical man; if he can't explain something, it isn't real. So my amazing stories and tales of Reiki were often met with a cynical smile.

The second day of the training was when the Reiki attunement took place. The attunement was a one to one session in Dee's spiritual room where she would enhance and awaken our abilities to use Reiki.

I sat on a chair; calm and gentle music was playing quietly. The room was lit with candles; if the chair hadn't been so uncomfortable I'd have been asleep in minutes. Dee performed the ritual by holding her palms over the parts of my aura called Chakras. The aura is the energy that surrounds our bodies – inside the aura are seven points that run down the centre of your body from the top of your head to the base of your spine. In Reiki it is believed the chakras spin and when the chakra becomes clogged it stops spinning properly. This is said to cause a range of physical symptoms around that particular chakra until Reiki is performed to rebalance the mind, body and spirit, allowing the chakra to spin to its natural function once more.

I had my eyes closed and felt Dee open my palms and gently tap the centre of them. My palms began to tingle all over. In my mind I saw mountains, behind which was beautiful blue water. On the mountain ledge I saw a fox curled around her cubs. This may sound as though I'm crazy but I assure you I'm quite sane and in my mind I definitely saw this.

After the attunement was complete Dee asked me if I saw anything – as though it was a frequent occurrence – which made me feel much better. When I told her what I saw she said it was the animal spirit world welcoming me. I have since learnt that the fox spirit represents, amongst other things, shape shifting; becoming someone or something new and I was; this was the beginning of my spiritual path.

Following my Reiki training I delved much deeper into the spiritual world and what I have found amazes me every day. I had numerous readings; in one a woman read my animal cards – a little like tarot but with the animal spirit guides - one of the things she said was that I was writing at the moment. I had started to write a memoir about my life, I hadn't told anyone but Dave about this. She told me it would be the first of many writing projects for me but this one would be the hardest emotionally. She said I was on the right path and if I was ever afraid I was just to ask for help and it would be given. This gave me the boost I'd been searching for. Now I knew I wasn't wasting my time and became determined that my story would one day find its way onto book shelves.

Chapter 21

New beginnings.

I loved where we lived. Our semi-detached house was on a modern estate; behind which was a walkway to a park. The park had a huge lake, fields, paths; it was dog walking paradise. Megan loved running free, playing with other dogs and it meant I got to talk to a lot of fellow dog lovers. It was the opposite with Ronnie and Tess of course where I actively avoided all contact with other dogs and people as they were still very taxing in that department. I was so happy to have my Megs; she made walking the dog what it should be and gave me what I yearned for from it; smiles, relaxation and company. Whenever Megan and I set off for our walk it would take us a while to even get to that park as a result of all the neighbourhood children wanting to stroke and talk to her. She dutifully gave them her paw when they asked for it - even after the tenth time – she never jumped up on them, just lapped up all the attention. It made me so proud to be her owner.

The house itself, however, was becoming a problem; in particular the stairs. Some days I'd stand at the bottom looking up at what seemed like a mountain. The fatigue meant whenever I climbed them I was left breathless, my heart pumping and my legs would be like jelly. So we made the sad decision to move to a bungalow. We also thought it would be a good idea to move a little closer to my mum, who was still making that long journey to see me every week and help me with any housework I couldn't manage.

So after lots of searching we found a two bedroom bungalow. Mum and Dad had generously said they would buy the bungalow and we could pay them rent. Finding a bungalow to rent privately in our price range had proved futile and coupled with the fact we had three dogs meant no landlord would touch us anyway. So this was a perfect solution; for Dave and I. Mum and Dad however had to add a lump sum to their mortgage in order to do this for us so we certainly owed them a debt; literally.

The bungalow was on a quiet street and there was a dog walk across the road where Megan could run off the lead. The move took its toll on me and I was having another attack. This time, whenever I leant my head forwards, an electric shock type pulse ran through the trunk of my body down to my legs. MS; to tell you the truth I still hadn't really dealt with it. I suppose in the back of my mind part of me still thought one day I'd wake up and it would have disappeared. It's because the constant fatigue becomes normality so it's not until I have an attack I'm reminded of the severity of the illness. The fact is that any day I could wake up and my life could be changed forever. Because the disease attacks the nerves, literally any part of my body could be affected; my legs, my eyesight, my ability to think. The thought of the control MS has over what my life will or will not be is terrifying; so I don't think about it, often.

I was having a really low day, the relapse and the reminders it brought had filled me with frustration and fear. On top of that we were struggling with money which was causing tension between me and Dave. I got up to discover the fridge had broken; all the food was ruined and I didn't have a clue how we were going to afford a new one. Oh no, I'd have to make the phone call to Dave, who was already under so much pressure money wise; it was a mess. I sat at the dining table and began to cry. Ronnie hopped up onto my knee as he often does; he then licked my nose, sneezed in my face, broke wind very loudly and after turning round to sniff his work, hopped off. The tears turned to hysterical laughing, Ronnie stood in front of me hopping on his front legs clearly happy with his job. Dogs; they really are the best medicine.

- - - - -

After the attack tapered off - a couple of weeks later - I felt so much better in day to day life. The freedom having a bungalow for a home gave me was unexpected. I had so much more energy without battling the stairs every day. As we prepared for Christmas, things began to settle down for me, health wise, for the first time in a year.

The fatigue was still an unwelcome lodger in my life but I seemed to be coping better. I was able to take on the role of house wife by doing just a little something each day. I walked the dogs but had to rest for an hour or so before attempting anything else, but still I didn't feel quite so useless. I was still keeping my saturated fats to a minimum. The times I did, inevitably, indulge in that cream cake or chocolate bar I'd feel the effects in my energy levels for the next week. It was clear that there was some standing in the diet; it's just sometimes, only chocolate will do. I am and always have been my own worst enemy.

After we put up our Christmas tree I lined up the three musketeers for a photo. As difficult as it was to have three dogs, especially with MS, just the sight of their little faces each day made everything seem a bit brighter. Whenever I was drained after attempting to do something around the house and collapsed on the sofa; there was always a warm body to snuggle into for comfort. They each had their own ways of making me smile. Megan was so gentle and loving that just her presence beside you filled you with warm feeling. Tessie would hop up next to me and sing her little song until I covered her in the blanket hanging on the back of the sofa. Ronnie, well, there's a wealth of material that boy does to make me laugh.

– – – – –

I went to see Denise and Dale at the kennels as often as I could; it was so nice to keep in touch, even if it was hard to be reminded of what I'd lost.

During one of my visits something came up which had been on my mind for a while.

"So when you going to get that dog bred then?" Dale asked referring to Megan. When I'd bought her, Dale had said she would have beautiful pups and that I was not to spay her. I'd said to Dave I would breed with her when I got her; it was what convinced him to let me have her in the first place. Having two dogs wasn't cheap; especially when I bought them new dog beds every time I entered a pet shop. Having Megan was, as he saw it, an expense we couldn't afford; and that was when I was still earning a wage. Now I had

Megan and loved her to the extent I did; breeding was suddenly a different ball game. I'd read up on the subject extensively and found all the risks involved to the bitch. There was the risk of caesarean should she have difficulty getting the puppies out. One of the puppies could die inside her during pregnancy and should the placenta become detached she, and the rest of the pups, could be poisoned and die. After the birth there was the risk of infection in the womb and mammary glands and there was a condition called eclampsia due to low calcium levels, which if not caught in time, could take Megan's life. As a result of all my Google activity I decided I really couldn't risk anything happening to her, I wouldn't do it. During my visit to Dale's I told him all of this.

"Arhhh don't be daft, if all that stuff happened a lot do you think I'd be running a breeding kennels? In some cases it happens, yeah, they have to write about it don't they? But it's very rare and I'd say you are more than prepared after all your bloody reading to see a vet in time if it did, aren't you?"

I smirked back at him as he mocked my excessive worrying. "Yes of course I would get her to a vet if anything was wrong. I don't know; I'm going to think about it a bit more, but thank you, you have made me feel better about the whole thing."

There was also the MS to think about. If I had an attack I wouldn't be able to take care of Megan and the puppies. Dave would be at work during the day and too tired to do much in the evenings. Though I knew I would take care of them anyway and I would probably end up in hospital. Should I let MS run my life? No definitely not, but at the same time the risk was there.

I thought of nothing else for months and in the end Megan made my mind up for me.

She'd had two seasons so far. After both seasons she's had what's known as a phantom pregnancy. This is when the hormones kick in around the time she would have given birth; basically their body thinks it's pregnant when it's not. Some cases of this are worse than others with some even producing milk. Thankfully Megan's was a mild case but tugged on my heart strings just the same.

She had a cuddly cat toy. It was a pink child's puppet to be exact, which meowed the tune of 'twinkle twinkle little star', and yes I do realise how sad that sounds now. Nonetheless she loved this toy the same way any dog loves their favourite toy. However, around the times she would have given birth, had I mated her, she never let this cat out of her sight. If she came up on the sofa, the cat came too. When she was eating her dinner, her cat was beside her bowl. She would lay and 'groom' it for hours each day and when it meowed as she picked it up, she would drop it and nudge it as if checking it was ok. After a few weeks her obsession with the cat would simply go back to the way it was before her season, until the next season came. It was the cutest thing and it made me feel terrible; who was I to take the experience of being a mum for real away from her? I agonised between the health risks and the morality of taking a womb away from a clearly maternal dog. In the end I decided to leave it up to her; I'd line up a mating for her and if she wanted to do it great, if she didn't, also great and I'm sure she would let the male dog know in no uncertain terms if he was not welcome around her rear end. So; all that was left to do was find my beautiful girl the perfect mate.

Chapter 22

Megan's a mummy.

Dale had a stud dog but unfortunately this was Megan's father and even in dogs that is definitely not ok. So I began the hunt on the internet. There were so many but none as close to home as I wanted. One day whilst visiting my local pet shop I decided to place a 'stud dog wanted' ad on the notice board. Within an hour I received a phone call from a breeder only ten minutes drive from me. He had an experienced stud dog called Bill, yes Bill, he clearly he wasn't your usual pretentious dog breeder, so I made an appointment to take Megan down and meet them both.

I wasn't comfortable going to meet a strange man on my own, so I waited for Dave to get home and we all went together; I took Megan with me to cast her approval. It was dark when we pulled up at the big wire gate. Inside the gate I could see a German shepherd dog bouncing off the walls of his kennel run. He was clearly very good at his job; his barks vibrated through the car. A man who looked around forty years old, I noted his age appearance as on the phone he'd sounded much older, opened the gate and signalled us on to the concrete driveway.

"Hello there you must be Emma, I'm Tom," the man said as we got out of the car. Dave introduced himself and we stood talking for what seemed like forever; it was freezing cold and all Dave and I wanted to do was sit down and chat over a nice warm cup of tea. The man did not invite us in however, nor did he show us around his kennels; I thought this odd as Dale never would have behaved this way. Dale was always the perfect host to his guests whether they were using his stud dog, booking dogs into the kennels or buying his puppies. So this sort of behaviour seemed more than rude to me but I suppose each man runs his business in his own way. He seemed genuine and once he showed us Bill, the bond they clearly had extinguished any worries niggling at me.

Bill was a lemon roan Cocker Spaniel (tan and white in non breeders' terms). He was very handsome and responded to every command Tom gave to him with enthusiasm and happiness. When he came over to me he reminded me of Megan; so polite but with a hint of Cocker craziness. Tom suggested Megan should meet Bill so we released her from the car where she'd had her nose pressed up against the window eager to be in on the fun. The two dogs ran around and played together, Megan clearly like him and Bill liked Megan, especially her rear end. So there it was – the perfect match. Megan wasn't due to be in season for a couple of weeks so we left it that I could bring Megan down when she was at the right point in her cycle and have her mated.

– – – – –

As I drove back to the breeding kennels a few weeks later I had butterflies. Not the good kind; the feeling as though you may be sick kind. I looked down at Megan sat beside me in the passenger seat – she had her own seatbelt – and my heart ached. I wish I could tell her what was going to happen, explain that if she didn't want to she didn't have to (though I'd be lying if I said I didn't say it all to her anyway). Tom met me at the gates again; Dave was at work so it was just us girls this time. I'm pretty sure Tom thought I was a complete idiot. I had stressed numerous times over the phone and in person that I was not interested in forcing Megan to be mated and I wanted it to be her choice. To a man in the business of breeding dogs that must have sounded ridiculous but I didn't care; all that mattered to me was Megan.

Tom let Bill out and Megan thought running around playing was great fun; but Bob had other ideas. As an experienced stud dog he could clearly smell Megan was ripe for the picking and started trying to mount her. Megan, the inexperienced bitch, was having none of it. They ran round together a little longer before Megan stood for Bill. This is when the bitch moves her tail to one side and stands still to allow the dog to get on board to do his business. Tom rushed over and held Megan. I had said much earlier I didn't want Megan being held – this goes on a lot in breeding establishments and it's nothing short of dog rape. Clearly I didn't want any part of this for my Megan; I wanted this to be all her own choice. But Tom had explained that once the dogs become tied inside if Megan was to pull away and run off it would severely damage both the dogs internally. So we had compromised that after Megan had 'decided' he may hold her to protect the dogs from injury. But after Bill had begun his business Megan changed her mind but it was too late. This was the most awful experience of my life. Megan made a horrific sound; a cross between a howl and a scream. I stroked her and she eventually calmed down and then it was over; Bill hopped off and that was the end of the most horrific memory I have. I paid Tom and took my baby girl home. I cried all the way and said I was sorry as I stroked her head.

Sometimes knowing what to do for the best morally for your dog is an impossible task. Had I taken her womb away I would have had to live with the question of how I'd feel if a more evolved race took my womb from me. So I tried to let Megan make up her own mind – which to a safe extent I did, she stood for the dog – but the reality of it was that she hadn't known what she was letting herself in for and neither had I. Still, it was done now but never again would I put any of my dogs through this; I just hoped she was pregnant so all this would have been worth it.

– – – – –

About three weeks later I took Megan for a scan at the vets. I couldn't be in the room with her but when they brought her out they informed me she was most certainly pregnant with at least three puppies but probably more it was hard to tell. I felt like a proud mum I was so happy. From then on Megan got only the best; freshly cooked chicken, mince, expensive dog food, pampering on the sofa and gentle ball throws instead of the usual rigorous walk.

I read every available bit of literature on nursing pregnant bitches. I ordered numerous books from Amazon and soaked up every piece of advice Dale and Denise gave me. I had all the supplies ready; bottles and formula in case any of the pups wouldn't feed from Megan, vet bedding, a whelping box and puppy run kindly made by

106

my brother's hands who was a very skilled joiner. The whelping box had a rail around the edge to prevent the pups being squashed against the sides by Megan. I had my birthing box; full of towels, buckets for water, scissors to cut cords in case Megan didn't know what to do and gloves. So by the end of Megan's nine week term (if only our pregnancies were that short) everything was ready for the arrival; including Megan who was enormous. If you placed your hands on her tummy you could feel the puppies moving inside; it was truly amazing and my eyes watered every time.

The day of the birth Megan slept a lot. I checked her temperature as there is said to be a rise in the bitch's body temperature the day of the birth, and Megan's was indeed higher than normal. Dale had warned me that the mother almost always delivers at night so not to expect any sleep when the time came.

I had set up the spare room with a single bed and the whelping box so I could be with her in the weeks around the birth; I didn't want her to cope with any of it alone. Dave and I stayed up until around midnight to see if Megan would start delivery but she simply lay there sleeping soundly. So I went to bed with Megs in the spare room and Dave settled down for the night with Ronnie and Tess in our room. I hadn't been in bed ten minutes when I heard Megan scratching and scooping her bedding; Dale had said this was called nesting and when she does this it wouldn't be long before you see a puppy. I turned on the light and went to sit next to her, I'd read the nesting time could last hours so I wasn't too panicked. Then I saw Megan licking at her vulva and panting – a lot. Then I saw a bulge emerging;

"Dave! Dave! Wake up she's started get in here!" A few seconds later Megan calmly pushed out a small sack and began immediately licking and pulling at the sack to allow the puppy to emerge and breathe. I was gobsmacked that Megan just knew what to do. As soon as she had the puppy breathing she began chewing at the umbilical cord; I simply flapped around with the scissors in my hand utterly redundant as my clever girl had it all under control. The puppy was so tiny; its pink tongue began to move and it squeaked as Megan licked his tan fur clean and dry. I'd checked the sex and Megan's first puppy was a beautiful boy. Then Megan began what looked as though she was rolling on him. I thought perhaps she was trying to get him to suckle as this is the first thing a pup should do to bond with his mother and get his suckling reflex going. I moved the pup onto her teat but he wouldn't attach; I squeezed Megan's teat but no milk came out. Megan seemed stressed and moved away and tried to roll on him again.

"She's trying to kill him, she doesn't have any milk, quick get the formula," I said to Dave, my voice laced with panic. I didn't know if she was trying to kill him at all, it could have all perfectly natural for all I knew but I wasn't taking any risks. Dave kept cool as a cucumber as usual and handed me the bottle; he wouldn't suckle from that either.

Dave had phoned my best friend Kerry an hour ago. Kerry was like my big sister and she loved Megan and all my dogs almost as much as me. When she'd asked if she could be here it was an easy yes. I'd warned her it would be a ridiculous hour but I was so happy to see her as she poked her head round the whelping room door. She could tell I was panicking so helped me place the puppy in the box I'd prepared, lined with a heat pad for the birth times when Megan would be scooping bedding. Megan began whelping her next puppy who was a chocolate girl with a white smudge on her nose. I tried again to place the puppy on her teat and this time the chocolate girl began suckling vigorously which Megan seemed quite happy with. So I took the little tan boy from his heat pad and placed him on a teat next to the other puppy – he suckled. We all let out a sigh of relief as I checked the other teats and milk appeared. I offered my poor girl some fresh water and endless love and reassurance. Aside from panting heavily she seemed to take it all in her stride and over the next three hours another four perfect puppies arrived; a tan and white boy, a solid chocolate girl, a solid tan girl and a tan and white girl. Megan rested as her beautiful babies suckled on her – she fell asleep for short times but would wake to check on each puppy. When I took them one by one to weigh them Megan would count them as I put them back; nudging each one to check they were ok.

Six, I thought, that must be it now, but I had a niggle. Megan would settle but then sit up and begin panting, as she had with the other births, but then go to sleep again as if content with her puppies.

I felt her tummy and was sure I felt another puppy move. I left it two hours as Dale had said to allow three in-between puppies before worrying. I felt again after then and felt nothing. I decided to ring the vets and take her down – it was a Sunday so the charges would be ridiculous but I didn't care. Megan was worth the world to me and a stuck puppy could be dangerous; for mum and pup. Just as Dave and I were getting ready to leave – all the puppies had to come too as Megan would get stressed separated from them even for half an hour – Megan began giving birth again. This time I insisted on helping her; she was tired and I had a bad feeling about this. We freed the pup from the sac and Megan and I cut the cord as a joint effort; but the puppy was cold and lifeless. I wrapped the chocolate boy in a towel and began rubbing and swinging him to try and instigate breathing but to no avail. Megan was going crazy trying to see the puppy, but I'd seen on you tube a mother ate her dead puppy and I certainly didn't want to see that – mainly though I didn't want her to have to see her dead baby. Dave said I should let her sniff him so I placed him in front of her nose; Megan nudged desperately at him until I took him away as we rushed to the vets.

The experienced vet listened for a heart beat but shook his head.

"I'm sorry but there's nothing I can do for this one. Let's have a look at the rest and mum." My heart dropped; I'd hoped there was some magical thing he could do to bring Megan's last baby back. But I had to be strong I had Megan and her litter to think about. So I wrapped the cold little boy up in the yellow towel I brought him in and covered his head before handing him over to Dave while I held Megan on the table for a check up. The good news was that mum and remaining six puppies were healthy; he gave Megan an injection to flush out any debris from the births and another to keep her calcium levels up.

On the way home I turned to Dave in the driver's seat.

"Can we bury him in the garden?" I had tears in my eyes.

"Course we can I'll do it soon as we get home while you get these guys settled."

Dave came into the room where I'd finally got mum and pups comfy and all were sleeping contently.

"Do you want to come and say anything before I cover him over?" Kerry stayed with Megan for me while I went outside. As I looked into the deep hole with the yellow towel at the bottom the tears flowed.

"We should give him a name, how about Frankie?" Dave laid a hand on my shoulder.

"Yeah, that's lovely, thank you," I placed my hand over his. "Night night little Frankie, I'm sorry I let you down little man." I just kept thinking if I'd gone to the vets sooner maybe we could have got him out alive.

I spoke to Dale later that day and he said not to be daft and that there's nearly always a dead one. He also said I should prepare myself to lose at least one more as this was likely to happen due to many things; Megan laying on them, them not getting enough milk, organs failing. No, I thought. No way was I going to let any more of Megan's babies die.

Chapter 23

Puppy days.

I heard the familiar squeaks of the puppies. I opened my eyes and felt around for my phone. It was pitch black; I pressed the button on my phone to reveal the light and time; 1: 24 am. I got out of bed and shone the light over the whelping box. Megan's big brown eyes stared back at me. 1, 2, 3, 4, 5, 6; I did the head count and went back to bed, until 3:36 am, 5:17 am and so on. My nights went on like this for about two weeks but I still had one healthy mummy and six alive and well puppies and that was the important thing. I, however, was exhausted. The fatigue was becoming overwhelming; but the amazing experience of puppy rearing was keeping me going. Many times I'd got out of bed to find the puppy who was squeaking was the big tan and white boy. He'd be stuck under the whelping rail trying to find mum but having no luck. Puppy's eyes don't open until they are around two – three weeks old. I'd pick him up and place him next to her where he lay contentedly suckling. This particular pup was so vocal Dave and I aptly named him Squeaker.

As soon as all the pups had their eyes open I relocated them to the kitchen into the puppy run. I put the whelping box in there too and Dave made them some little steps for them to get in and out. It was adorable watching them stumble around. The kitchen was only across the hall from our bedroom so I was still up and down in the night a few times but I was getting a little more rest.

Megan loved being a mummy. She groomed them, counted them, and lovingly nudged them each time they cried and snuggled down with them all to keep them warm. I had to practically drag her out for a wee, after which she would run back to the door to be reunited with her babies. As the days turned into weeks and the puppies had started to grow teeth; Megan was less enthusiastic to be in the pen with them. The pups would constantly be trying to feed so I decided it was time for weaning. Pups are weaned onto food at around five weeks old; Megan's pups were only four but Dale had said it would do no harm to start early.

I had been so undecided on whether breeding Megan was the right thing to do; for both me and her. I had coped unexpectedly well with the work load but I'd be lying if I said it hadn't taken its toll. But the experience of bringing new life into the world and watching and nurturing their development was one of the best experiences of my life. Megan was an exceptional dog; she had and still was; helping me get through some really tough times by just being the amazing being she was. Mating her meant her line would be carried on through her puppies; maybe one day one or all of them would help their owners the way Megan inspires me. So the mating had been an awful part of it but seeing Megan with her babies everyday; she was in her element. It is the most natural thing in the world for any female – whatever the species – to become a mother, and I'm so glad now that I didn't take away that opportunity for Megan. Breeding dogs is a very controversial issue in our present society; with due cause. We are over populated with dogs but I stand firmly by the fact that the world needs dogs like Megan and that her breed; typically, are not the ones stuck in rescue centres unable to find homes.

If Megan had been a Staffordshire bull terrier I wouldn't have even thought about breeding her. And yes that is hypocritical as female staffies deserve to be mums just as much as Megan did. The difference being that I know, from volunteering in rescues, that staffies make up a large percentage of the dogs. They are also used as statement dogs for people who don't respect or love them. Bringing puppies in to the world comes with responsibility and I couldn't be sure one of the puppies wouldn't become one of the large statistics in rescues. And no I can't say Megan's puppies wouldn't end up in a rescue either; but I do know the world is crying out for spaniels and they wouldn't be waiting long.

The hype surrounding staffies is so frustrating. The breed in general is loyal, gentle and loving. The kennel club recommends them as being one of the best breeds to have with children. But somewhere along the line the press have formed a bandwagon demonising the breed. Staffies are not the only breed to 'turn' on a child or adult, they are just the only ones that sell papers. Dogs simply communicate in a different ways and if we want to share our home with them, it's our responsibility to speak and listen to their language as well as expecting them to learn ours.

This was so clear to me when I watched Megan's pups. Their innate behaviour was incredible to watch. I'd always heard that in a litter of pups there is a hierarchy and that this will be the pup's pack role for the rest of their life. I was very sceptical about this; they are a litter of puppies after all, just weeks old. I do, however, have to say it really does have some standing.

The puppies would be playing and it would nearly always end up in little growls and snarls; they'd be biting one another and standing on each other's backs. This is classic dominance; putting themselves above the other one – asserting their strength. Before long I began to see a clear difference in terms of hierarchy between the puppies, especially the more dominant ones.

I had been very lucky in finding homes for Megan's babies; all but one had wonderful homes to go to when they were ready.

Firstly we had Alfie – the first born – he was huge. If there was trouble to be found Alfie was there. If there was fighting going on Alfie would usually have started it; and if he hadn't he'd certainly finish it. He was definitely top of the pack, and was always letting everyone else know it; taking toys, muscling in on food and cuddles and never ending play fighting. Despite being hard work Alfie was adorable – he was a beautiful deep tan colour and had a face that always said 'what me?'. Alfie was Megan's favourite; she loved playing with him.

Alfie was going to a young couple who had just bought their first house, they regularly looked after their family dogs and when asked what they'd do if Alfie ruined anything, they said it wouldn't matter as long as he was ok. They fell in love with him when they came to see him and he fell asleep in the man's arms.

Next in the hierarchy we had Daisy. Daisy was the female version of Alfie and they were constantly battling it out for top dog. But she was beautiful; all brown with a white smudge on her nose. She was so loving, and when they all snuggled up together all fights were forgotten as they nuzzled into one another. A family from Kent had chosen Daisy; I was a little heartbroken as I'd really taken to her and secretly had wondered what it would be like to keep her (even though 'we weren't keeping any'). But the family were lovely and the two children loved Daisy. I warned them that having a puppy was hard work and challenging but they assured me they were up to the job.

Then we had Bonnie; a tan and white girl. Bonnie's owner had been the first to respond to the advert and she had chosen Bonnie from a photo when she was only two weeks old. I had felt really good about Bonnie's owner from the moment I'd spoken to her. She had recently lost someone very close to her and had been drawn to Bonnie. This was what I had wanted from breeding; for Megan's puppies to carry on her amazing emotional supportive nature. Bonnie was a middle to lower ranking pup, she minded her own business but would defend herself whenever one of the others tried to dominate her. All the puppies were gorgeous but Bonnie really was true to her name; dainty and beautiful. They were a perfect family with two children; they lived right next to Richmond Park in London where Bonnie would enjoy daily walks.

Fern's owner had waited a long time for her. I often went into the local pet shop with Megan to get supplies and one of the staff had fallen in love with her. So when she'd heard I was breeding Megan she was first in line to say she would take one. Unfortunately she had wanted a chocolate brown boy to go with her existing one; sadly Frankie the pup that passed away was the only chocolate boy. So when Sue and her husband came to view the puppies they had open minds. Fern was almost as big as the boys; light fawn in colour and had the most beautifully placid temperament. I loved Fern; she was by far the most similar to Megan in temperament. This swung it for them and they fell for her.

Now Bailey, aka squeaker, was Dave's favourite. But my brother and his girlfriend, after much bombarding, had chosen to take him. Bailey hated being on his own; hence the constant squeaking whenever his friends were playing or sleeping without him. He was – despite his large size – a lower rank in the pack, preferring a cuddle over play fighting or gaining dominance. My brother was going to take him to work with him so he would always be close by to his new friend. He was a light fawn colour like fern with white markings on his chest and tummy. His paws reminded me of a bear's; they were huge.

Last but not least we had Ruby. Ruby was the smallest of the pack and right from the get go she was the lowest ranking pup. I'd have to regularly monitor her weight to ensure she was getting enough milk as the others would push her out the way. But she quickly caught up despite being the smallest. She would play with the others but I rarely saw her fighting for dominance. Ruby hadn't been chosen by any of the people who had come to see the litter. She was all chocolate brown apart from four white socks on her feet. She was so cute; the perfect tiny package. We called her 'mini Megs' as her coat markings and small size reminded us of Megan as a puppy. I have no doubt I could have found her a home eventually; but I'd already taken it as fate that Ruby should join our pack.

We'd agreed; Dave and I – that I wouldn't keep any of the puppies - three dogs was enough. But from the moment I saw them I loved each and every one. Whilst I was happy I'd found them wonderful loving homes; I couldn't help but yearn to keep one. I also felt unexpectedly guilty taking all Megan's babies away. Dale had said that Dogs weren't like humans – they loved being a mum for a while but then detached themselves. To a certain extent Megan had done this during the weaning; she wanted to be back with her own pack most of the time, she'd still go and check on them but she grew happier to leave them. That was until she discovered how fun it was to play with them. She was the perfect balance of playmate and mum; putting them in line if they bit too hard or got too excited. She really was incredible with them and I couldn't take them all away could I?

No I couldn't. The last little brown girl became part of pack Coldron. I can't take any of the credit for integrating this defenceless tiny puppy into a pack with two aggressive Jack Russells once again. Dave was amazing; I walked in one day to find Ruby running around the lounge with Ronnie and Tess lying down dutifully. A day later I heard playing coming from the other room and Ronnie and Ruby were playing chase. How he did it I don't know but his calm assertive demeanour probably had a lot to do with it.

Soon the time came for the rest of the puppies to go to their new homes. I won't say it wasn't emotional for both me and Megan. But we both had Ruby to keep us busy, the two of them would play for hours in the garden then come and snuggle up together; so I definitely made the right decision.

Little Daisy came back to us for a short time. The family were heartbroken to have to bring her back but the daughter was scared of Daisy's puppy biting. I explained this would pass and gave them tips but she ended up back in my arms anyway. So I made sure the next people would be the right ones. Daisy went to live with a couple with teenage children and a cocker spaniel from Birmingham. The man of the family's job was putting up stages at festivals and events. He explained his current dog came everywhere with him and he planned the same for Daisy. So she would spend her days running around fields and never far away from her owner. I still receive messages and photos saying how happy they are with her. So it just goes to show, sometimes fate finds a way.

I also receive updates from all the other pups and it's lovely to see how they have grown and developed into members of their families.

Chapter 24

The future.

We settled into life with four dogs and it really wasn't much more work than three. Other than having my heart in my mouth whenever Ruby tried to play with Ronnie or Tess, plus the puppy chewing, oh and the toilet training which wasn't going as well as I'd expected; ok so it was a lot more work but she was worth it.

As for my health it was up and down; down being more the norm than up. My consultant was concerned my medication wasn't working so he's put me on another; and it was awful. The new meds gave me aches and pains like I had the flu and the actual injections were agony. Every three days I had to go through this and it was reminding me just how awful it was to have MS. As if the actual disease wasn't bad enough now I had to inject myself with pain. The first meds had been great; no pain (well very minimal) no aches, in fact no side effects whatsoever, they just weren't strong enough for me.

So I grinned and bared it, and I have to say two months later my symptoms were a lot more controlled. The medication, I'm told, doesn't help the fatigue but it helps reduce the relapses. So I was still living with the fatigue but I was coping with it in my own way. Whenever had a low day I would snuggle up on the sofa with a blanket and my four wonderful dogs.

Ruby was the sweetest thing; she had so many adorable traits. She was six months old now and was growing into a beautiful dog. She wasn't at all like Megan in temperament though, Megan was very chilled and placid; Ruby definitely had her dad's working spirit. If I didn't keep her occupied she would find her own entertainment in the form of de – stuffing all the toys, aggravating the other dogs to play and doing laps of the house at full speed. But as I say, other than that no extra work at all. She also was very clingy which I admit I encouraged; I liked being followed around and missed when

I wasn't there. If I ever saw something shocking on the telly and took a sharp intake of breath; Ruby would rush over and rest her head on my shoulder as if comforting me – just adorable. Megan loved her baby too, Dave took Ruby out one day on her own and Megan never left the window waiting for her to come back, we never separate them now. If I take one out with me the other comes along too. So even though it was extra work for me, it felt as though our doggie family was complete now – four was most definitely enough.

The calm after the madness of breeding was both welcome and unnerving. It had been such hard work but I'd loved having a purpose again, and now, despite having a very busy time with four dogs; I felt something was missing. I knew what it was; this hole had been there since I left the kennels. I missed working so much. Whenever I started looking for jobs though, I'd come down with another attack or my fatigue would be crippling. I had to be realistic; what employer would want someone who would probably be off sick every few weeks? It had to be something in my control. Since I'd been unemployed Mum had been telling me to write. I had started a while ago, after the wedding, but it had gone on the back burner during puppy days. So I sat in front of my laptop once again. During my psychic reading I'd been told the spirits would help me complete this task and I truly felt they were helping me now. I couldn't type the words fast enough sometimes, others I'd be staring at the screen willing them to come. But one thing was for sure; writing was the way forward for me. It had to be. On my good days I could manage up to a couple of hours; and when I was having a bad day I could curl up and relax without the pressure of ringing in sick or letting anyone down. So life continued but I had something to work towards.

– – – – –

Dave and I had always been in rented houses, so when my parents sold their house and offered us the deposit to buy our own place we were ecstatic. My parents were incredible for even thinking of doing that for us. So after seeing the mortgage advisor and being approved the search began for our new home once again – but this time it came

118

with both the excitement of it being ours and the responsibility and fears that came with owning a house.

There was an awful lot of pressure on Dave money wise. Since I'd had to give up work, it had been a struggle to say the least. There were a lot of rows about money, or more the lack of it. I often felt like a burden. Having MS came hand in hand with a lack of independence for me and I'm sure many others with the disease. I've read so many cases where MS has driven relationships apart. The shift in the partnership where one has to become a carer can drive a wedge between a couple. For us most of the problem was the way I thought. I felt like less of a person because I needing looking after, I felt less attractive to Dave because he had to treat me like a dependent child sometimes. I felt like a waste of space because we were struggling so much money wise and I couldn't do anything about it. But I tried to remember I had my writing and the hope that maybe one day I could contribute to my marriage money wise once again. I'd always loved to read and was a definite book worm; I was also very good at English back in school. So writing was a way to channel everything I was going through with a hope that maybe one day someone would read my story and think it was worth publishing. I also had the hope that perhaps I could become who I had been, instead of feeling like a patient every day of my life. Don't get me wrong I did love my life; I had an amazing husband, my four wonderful dogs, special friends and the best family a girl could wish for, but I just wanted to feel normal again. My brother and his girlfriend had just had their first baby; Bethany. So now I was an aunty and I loved every second with the new member of the family, it had though, brought back that niggling wish for a baby of my own.

Dave and I had talked about what our kids would be like from the very beginning of our relationship, it was always on the cards; then I got MS.

Since diagnosis we had spoken about having children at great length. There was obviously the point of having the disease and being a mother. At first Dave just said there was no way he could manage; looking after me, the dogs and a baby when he got in from a day's hard labour was an understandably daunting thought. But after many discussions and a lot more thinking we decided that having a baby was something we desperately wanted and letting MS take that away from us just wasn't something we could let happen. So amongst the house hunting, dog walking, writing and MS management we began trying to become pregnant. I had to come off my medication while we were trying to conceive as the doctors didn't know what it could do to a developing foetus.

Having a baby was going to be difficult for me to manage with the dogs and the illness. So we decided to move to the small village where my parents and brother lived, at least then I would have my support network around me. After seeing a few bad properties we found our new home; a two bedroom semi-detached house. I'd had my heart set on another detached bungalow; the dogs barked a lot and I had found no stairs so much easier with my fatigue. But after scouring the net for months, I'd accepted that our funds just couldn't stretch that far. The house was gorgeous though. It had a big kitchen, dining room and lounge downstairs and upstairs the second bedroom was already a beautiful nursery.

I admit I had severely underestimated how stressful buying a house was. With Dave working all the hours God sent, most of the admin and phone calls were left to me. People often think that the fatigue MS sufferers cope with is only affected by physical exercise. This isn't the case – well not with me anyway. Physical activity did affect me severely if I didn't rest in-between doing things. What I don't think some people understand is how draining it is just to have a conversation. Using your brain requires energy too. You will know this if you have ever gone without sleep all night and then have to cope the next day at work. You make mistakes, mix up your words and forget things. This is every day for me. When I have a friend over for a few hours I feel as though I've run a marathon and often sleep for hours afterwards. So being on and off the phone all day, concentrating on filling out forms, changing addresses and sorting out insurances for the new place definitely took its toll.

I had a string of attacks affecting my balance, numbness in my feet and pain in my eyes. But there really was no choice but to carry on best I could.

After what felt like an eternity we got the keys for our first owned property. After the commotion of moving Dave and I stood in each other's arms.

"Well, this is ours then," Dave smiled at me; his face inches from mine.

"Yep, look at us all grown up and committed – married, mortgage, trying for a baby – who would have thought it all those years ago?" I smiled back and my lips met his.

We'd come through so much and I felt like thanks to him and my family, I was still moving forwards, despite the MS pulling me back hard.

I know our first house is just the beginning. One day we will live in that beautiful white cottage in the middle of a field, with no neighbours to annoy. I'll have a big garden for the dogs and a veggie patch where me and our little boy or girl will plant seeds and watch them grow. We will all go for walks in the country and I'll teach my child all about the beauty of nature. Until that dream comes true though, we live in our beautiful little house, on a street in a quiet village, close to family. I get to take my dogs beautiful country walks every day.

It's amazing how having something like MS makes you appreciate the smaller things in life. I thank my lucky stars every day for the use of my legs, the fact I can see, hear and talk. I love every second I spend with my wonderful husband (apart from the endless list of bad habits every man possesses of course!). I appreciate my family and friends more and make them my priority.

I found a rescue centre a few miles from me and, on my good days, I love to go and help out once a week if I can. I love to shower the homeless dogs with love and affection; but above all I love feeling a part of something again. There is a wonderful team of people there with an exceptional woman at the head of it all; they all understand my limitations without pity and I never feel pressured to go. The weeks I'm poorly I'm wished well and welcomed back weeks or months later, with welcome arms. So even though I lost Pond View kennels; I found a small place in the canine world for a girl whose body lets her down but whose love of dogs grows each day.

I owe the canine species a great debt. Having my dogs has got me through the toughest times in my life. Yes the Jack Russels have been extremely hard work but they make me smile every day. Ruby and Megan offer endless love and affection. If I'm ever down, one of them if not both are always by my side to offer warmth and those big brown eyes that say; 'I love you mum'. We are still trying for our baby, six months now, but we're not giving up. Hopefully before too long we will be graced by the pitter patter of tiny feet and all the joy and challenges a tiny Coldron will bring.

Looking back at my life three years ago, after diagnosis; I'm so proud of myself for how far I've come. There were times I wondered what the point of going on was; the disease would only ever get worse. But I fought back and found ways to cope and live once again.

I found Spirituality, a path I may never have turned down if it hadn't been for the trauma of diagnosis. I trained to get my Reiki qualification and took healing my body into my own hands. I married the love of my life and we have a wonderful home of our own. I helped to bring new life into the world with Megan and I have no doubt her offspring will be as incredible for their families as Megan is for ours. Now I work towards another goal; to be an accomplished writer. Being diagnosed with MS doesn't have to mean the end of your life; you may just get pushed in a new direction by it but perhaps it was where you were always meant to go.

I'd be lying if I said the fear of my MS progressing didn't still enter my thoughts daily and sometimes consume them. But with the help of everyone around me – including my beautiful dogs – when I find myself there I can find a way out of the darkness and in to the light.

I sit here now in my garden; my four dogs sleeping at my feet. The sun shines on my face and I smile. That's the thing about the sunshine you see; some days you can't feel its warmth or see its brightness, but it's always there. Then one day the clouds will clear...and there it will be.

Angels Don't Have Wings

Angels don't have wings, long robes and halos,
They have four legs, a tail and a shiny wet nose.
They don't sing choir songs all bathed in white light,
They lie by your side all through the night.
An angel is never far from your view,
If you look for them, they will find you.
When you need them the most they enter your life,
They'll shower you with love through your time of strife.
What they ask in return is nothing at all,
But a scratch behind the ear and the throw of a ball.
They'll rest a paw on your lap when a tear is shed,
They'll light up your eyes with a cock of their head.
No, angels don't have wings, long robes and halos,
They have four legs, a tail and a shiny wet nose.

Emma Coldron

References

Jelinek, G. (2010). Overcoming Multiple Sclerosis; An Evidence-Based Guide to Recovery. Lancaster, UK: Impala Books.